Upgrading labour market information
in developing countries:
Problems, progress and prospects

ISBN 92-2-106453-0

First published 1989

Photocomposed in India
Printed in Switzerland

ATA

Upgrading labour market information in developing countries: Problems, progress and prospects

L. Richter

A synthesis of the results of an
ILO/DANIDA inter-regional seminar

International Labour Office   Geneva

Preface

This volume has emerged from an inter-regional seminar held in Copenhagen in October 1986 within the framework of an International Labour Office (ILO) project financed by the Danish International Development Agency (DANIDA) on the upgrading of labour market information (LMI) systems in developing countries. This seminar followed a series of five tripartite regional seminars which aimed at bringing together high-level national delegations to discuss problems they were encountering, to exchange experiences and to enable them to learn what could be done to improve the situation. The tripartite regional seminars were organised for English- and French-speaking Africa, Asia and the Pacific, the Caribbean and Latin America. The major objective of the Copenhagen seminar was to draw lessons from the regional seminars and from experience of LMI in the different regions, and to examine the remaining key problems and the ways and means of solving them. A summary of the issues discussed, and the highlights which emerged, were published in a standard formal report in February 1987. As a complement to this report, it was decided to prepare the present study.

This study provides a comprehensive analysis based on the thematic papers discussed at the inter-regional seminar. It gives an overview of the development and progress of LMI which have taken place in developing countries over the past few years. It focuses on the limits of the methods and approaches used in generating and managing LMI, especially with regard to the urban informal sector and the employment implications of structural adjustment policies.

The author concludes by analysing the implications of sound labour market reporting systems for policy-oriented action and by focusing attention on the key areas and priorities for future technical co-operation activities in the fields of employment planning and policies.

Jean-Bernard Célestin

Employment Planning and
Population Branch,
Employment and Development
Department

Contents

Chapter 1

Introduction and background

A. The nature and scope of labour market information (LMI)

Although "labour market information" means nothing more nor less than what it says—information about labour markets—it is difficult, if not impossible, to arrive at a common understanding and definition of what the term really stands for. This is primarily due to the fact that the number of users of such information is large and that they have different requirements with regard to content, detail, frequency and timeliness of information delivery.[1] Another reason is that although many people do need and make use of labour market information in various ways, they are not quite familiar with the concept or care little about its exact meaning. They only take more interest in the subject if a specific item of labour market information which they would like to have is either unavailable or not "informative" enough to produce the knowledge desired.

The main users and purposes of labour market information may be briefly characterised as follows:[2]

National policy-makers and planners must know the current levels and composition of employment, unemployment and underemployment and be able to read their trends. In conjunction with other information, this provides an "informed" basis on which they can build sound strategies and policies to influence the evolution of the labour market with a view to balancing manpower supply and demand—now and in the future. The type of information demanded by these users ranges from general information on the current overall situation of manpower and employment, with some preview of future developments, to quite sophisticated forecasts and projections of future industry, occupational and geographical distribution.

Employers' and workers' organisations, too, have to rely on such information and, in particular, on facts and data regarding wage levels and differentials, labour turnover, productivity, manpower surpluses and shortages and cost-of-living indices. Without such data they will find it impossible to formulate their policies and standpoints realistically and effectively as regards public manpower and employment policies, in general, and collective bargaining and wage fixing, in particular.

Educational and vocational training planners, likewise, wish to obtain a clear picture of how labour demand and supply will look in the future, both in the long and short run. They feel that they must have this picture in considerable occupational detail in order to relate manpower development policies and programmes as closely as possible to assessed requirements.

Vocational guidance and orientation services constitute another important group of information users. They can only provide meaningful advice about job opportunities if they can rely on occupational information which is drawn from the regular observation and analysis of the performance and changing fortunes of different occupations or clusters/families of occupations.

Employment exchanges or services need to know where vacancies exist and are likely to arise and what the qualifications of jobseekers are. Fully equipped with such knowledge, they can help to accelerate matching processes and avoid waste of time and effort on the part of jobseekers and employers, and the economy at large.

Finally, all the individual and organised actors in the labour market and the wider public need to be informed of situations and developments in manpower supply and demand in their localities, travel-to-work areas and farther afield. This helps informed and rational decision-making and promotes equity in the search for employment and access to jobs. The quality of job choices of young people in their early stages of participation in the labour market is likely to benefit greatly from improved labour market information.

In order to meet and serve these varying needs and interests, labour market information output has to be comprehensive, accurate, timely, accessible and usable. A practical definition of the term "labour market information" could therefore be formulated in the following terms: "Any information concerning the size and composition of the labour market or any part of the labour market, the way it or any part of it functions, its problems, the opportunities which may be available to it, and the employment-related intentions or aspirations of those who are part of it."[3]

In developed countries labour market information systems largely meet these requirements by a multitude of labour market information sources. These are tapped by highly sophisticated and comprehensive statistical mechanisms operated with well-organised data collection, processing, analysis and dissemination techniques. Nevertheless, users keep complaining that they have "a hard time obtaining information in the form they need",[4] at the right time and in the necessary detail. On the whole, however, shortcomings in labour market information in these countries cannot be said to raise serious and unsurmountable problems.

The real problem seems to lie elsewhere. There is clear evidence from many industrialised countries that labour market information has given clearly and persistently strong signals about important and worsening imbalances in manpower supply and demand. On the other hand, it is equally clear that policy-makers either ignored these signals in favour of other policy priorities or did not respond to them to the extent required to deal with them substantially. The high rates of unemployment and its main features, including the social and occupational groups most affected, have been fully reported and analysed for many years. Their persistence can hardly be blamed on inadequate or faulty labour market information. Appropriate and committed policies—not information—have been the absent factor.

This problem is certainly not unknown to developing countries. In fact, it may be argued that chronic job shortages in these countries are so obvious that more labour market information merely adds to what is already known. However, there is no doubt that the state of knowledge of labour market functioning in these countries is less than satisfactory. Moreover, the socio-economic environment in which the labour market is working, the main issues with which it is confronted, the wide gap that exists between the actual and potential roles of labour market information as a decision-making instrument and the means and resources available to bring about needed improvements in relation to unfulfilled needs are basically different from those of the industrialised countries.

No more than about a decade ago, very few developing countries were in possession of a mechanism which produced more than a rudimentary portrayal of the labour market. At best, some basic aggregate information was available on the size and the broad composition of the national labour force derived from population censuses or estimates, supplemented by ad hoc manpower/establishment surveys and the activity records generated by weak employment services for the—numerically insignificant—formal wage-earning sector. The latter contained mainly vacancy notifications, registration of jobseekers and placement figures, with a minimum of analysis to which little attention was paid. All this made for a rather fragile information base. It should be recalled that it was on such shaky grounds that manpower planning was undertaken throughout the sixties, as the favourite adjunct of the major development planning concerns at that time, to accelerate economic growth and bring about rapid industrialisation.

B. Changing policies and their effects on LMI

The seventies saw a remarkable upsurge of interest in and concern with strengthening the labour market information capacity in developing countries, as those engaged in manpower planning had strongly suggested. However, the severe criticisms to which manpower forecasts and projections had fallen victim around this time make it hard to see that the driving force for this interest and concern originated from the information requirements of manpower planning. And, in fact, the main impulses came from elsewhere. During the fifties and sixties manpower forecasting and projections had thrived on the policy proposition that closely relating assessment of needs with the development of skilled manpower for economic growth and industrialisation, would accelerate and further this process. It was expected that ever-increasing levels of production, income and employment would almost automatically follow, with the often-cited "trickle-down" effect taking care of distributional and social equity objectives. When these expectations did not materialise, economic growth found itself "dethroned" in the early seventies as the major objective of socio-economic development policy. Its place was taken by the goals of employment promotion, a more equitable distribution of income and the elimination of poverty. With this reorientation of economic policy objectives, classical manpower planning also fell out of favour. However, it soon became apparent that the new policy orientations placed not only different but at the same time far greater claims on an already deficient manpower and employment information base.

The subsequent "basic needs" and "rural poor" variants of these new development policy orientations, which gained currency in the mid-seventies, re-inforced this trend towards expanding needs for manpower and employment data. By focusing attention on the problems and opportunities of the large number of poor and disadvantaged people, most of them engaged in informal sector activities, information needs extended from the national aggregate policy level to regional and local levels.

All these policy reorientations were staunchly supported and activated by the ILO World Employment Programme. This programme was essentially concerned with improving, through a vast research effort, the base of knowledge on which the new policies and strategies were to be founded. As part of this programme and prompted by the criticisms levelled against manpower planning of the forecasting type, a review was undertaken of the technical co-operation projects which the ILO had carried out in the field of manpower planning during the sixties and early seventies. The primary objectives of this exercise were to find out *(a)* what the projects had achieved in the light of the objectives assigned to them; *(b)* which major problems they had met and how they had coped with them; and *(c)* more generally, whether and in what way the criticisms made against manpower planning were corroborated by field experience. At the same time, it was expected that this assessment would yield advice and guidance regarding direction and emphasis which future ILO technical co-operation activities should take in the manpower planning field.

This review was started in 1975 in Asia.[5] It was subsequently extended to Africa, both English and French speaking and to Arab countries.[6] Similar assessments, though partly in different contexts and not exclusively related to ILO sponsored technical co-operation projects in the manpower planning field, also took place in the Pacific region, Latin America and the Caribbean.

The major conclusions and lessons which emerged from these assessments varied somewhat in substance and emphasis between the different regions. However, three findings and propositions can be singled out as being of general significance and relevance. The first was to de-emphasise forecasting and projection work and to be aware of its limitations; the second to pay more attention to information gathering and analysis of labour market situations, trends and notably imbalances between manpower supply and demand; and the third to carry manpower planning work into the so far grossly neglected informal sector, both in rural and urban areas. In order to assist developing countries to bring these main conclusions to bear on their respective efforts and programmes, all reviews argued strongly for the establishment by the ILO of a longer-term and flexible programme of technical co-operation. This should concentrate on upgrading labour market reporting capacity for a wide variety of decision-making purposes in the formulation, implementation and monitoring of manpower and employment policy. In response to these proposals, such a programme was initiated at the end of the seventies.

C. An ILO programme for upgrading LMI in developing countries—An inter-regional seminar in 1986 as its climax

The nature and scope of the programme and its major activities and outputs are presented in a summary account.[7] Six main components formed the backbone of the programme. While some of these are still in progress or have been modified, others have been completed. A culminating point, taking stock of progress and attempting to visualise the future, was a seminar component financed by DANIDA. This consisted of five regional seminars held for English speaking Africa in Nairobi (1983), for Asia in Bangkok (1984), for the Caribbean in Antigua (1985), for Latin America in Santiago (1985) and for French-speaking Africa in Abidjan (1986). The main objective of the seminars was *(a)* to bring about an exchange of national experience among senior personnel and staff concerned with labour market information activities in government agencies, as well as in employers' and workers' organisations, and *(b)* to provide a training ground for such personnel on the different steps to be taken in longer-term, priority-oriented and cost-effective national programmes to upgrade labour market information capacity for rational decision-making of the main actors in the labour market, i.e. governments and employers' and workers' organisations.

This series of regional seminars was followed by an inter-regional seminar, also financed by DANIDA and jointly organised by the ILO and the Danish Ministry of Labour in Copenhagen in 1986. The inter-regional seminar was entrusted with the task of undertaking a synopsis of the major lessons to be drawn from the five regional seminars. It was also expected to highlight the key issues—old and new—which have remained unresolved and needed to be addressed in the future, at national and international levels.

The main purpose of this publication is to provide an overview of the state of the art of LMI in developing countries, its broad lines of development since the inception of the ILO programme of "strengthening manpower and employment information for decision-making in the mid-seventies", of the issues ahead and the priority areas to be dealt with at national and international levels. It does not intend to be a report on the proceedings and on the outcome of the inter-regional seminar in the strict sense. While it draws quite extensively on the documents prepared for the seminar, as well as on their discussions, it is foremost concerned with presenting an overall forward-looking view, on the basis of general programme experience, of the key issues which need to be addressed in the future and the nature and scope of the action required. It proposes to do so by placing these issues in a continuum of retrospect and prospect.

It is obvious that because of its limitation to highlighting past, present and future issues regarding efforts to upgrade labour market information, this monograph cannot do full justice to the many informative and thought-provoking individual contributions made to the inter-regional seminar in the form of papers on particular issues, reports on follow-up missions, regional assessments and selected country studies.[8]

Notes

[1] UNDP/ILO: *Labour market information—Sri Lanka*, Technical Report, SRL/82/005 (Geneva, 1984), p. 2.

[2] L. Richter: *Labour market information in developing countries—A general review* (Geneva, ILO, 1978).

[3] P. Jones: "Labour market information programmes—Priority needs, constraints and opportunities in the Asian region", in ILO: *Labour market information in Asia—Present issues and tasks for the future* (Geneva, 1980).

[4] Michigan State University/Wayne State University: *On the feasibility of a labour market information system* (East Lansing, Michigan), Vol. 1, 1974, p. 9.

[5] ILO: *Manpower assessment and planning projects in Asia—Situation, problems and outlook* (Geneva, 1978).

[6] R. Castley: "Crisis in human resource planning in sub-Saharan Africa", in ILO/Jobs and Skills Programme for Africa (JASPA): *The challenge of employment and basic needs in Africa* (Nairobi, Oxford University Press, 1986), and ILO: *Manpower and assessment planning projects in the Arab region—Current issues and perspectives* (Geneva, 1979).

[7] ILO: *Strengthening manpower and employment information for decision making—A summary account of a new programme of technical co-operation* (Geneva, 1981).

[8] For the interested reader, a collection of these contributions can be obtained on request from a limited stock available at ILO/E/POPLAN.

Chapter 2

Progress in labour market information capacity in developing countries

A. An overall perspective

As already pointed out in the introduction, the considerable rise of concern for and interest in widening and improving the capacity of labour market information generation and analysis in developing countries since the early seventies is due to a number of reasons. Among these, disenchantment with the usefulness of conventional, manpower planning and the reorientation of development planning objectives from growth to employment, income distribution and poverty elimination have played a decisive role. These changed policy concerns have brought with them, in addition to drives for more diversified macro-level and aggregate manpower and employment information, a shift of demand towards more regularly collected, more detailed and more locally based information. This included, in particular, the reporting on situations, trends and employment opportunities in those sectors, occupational groups and regions which either had a large proportion of the target population of these policies or possessed the potential resources to be developed for the benefit of these target groups.

It became rapidly apparent that these new information requirements were substantial. Considering the low level and the weak basis of the existing labour market information set-up in many developing countries, there was no short cut to a well-planned, longer-term, step-by-step effort to upgrade labour market information to meet the most essential needs and requirements first. In other words, no dramatic improvements could be expected in upgrading of labour market information in the short run.

Nevertheless, there are several indications that notable progress has been made in an increasing number of developing countries. Regular population censuses, providing the basics about the national manpower resources of a country, have become a world-wide exercise. Moreover, household surveys at shorter intervals, which cast light on the more detailed composition of the labour force, of employment levels and of unemployment rates, have also become more numerous. The ILO *Year Book of Labour Statistics* gives evidence of slow, but steady progress in this respect. While in 1975, 15 developing countries relied on household surveys as providers of one of the most important indicators of the labour market situation—unemployment—this number had increased to 22 developing countries by 1984.[1] Trends in the number of ad hoc surveys and studies on specific labour market problems and issues have also been clearly upwards. Many of them have led to better insights into the difficulties experienced by social or occupational groups who are particularly vulnerable to labour market imperfections. At the same time, statistics published by the employment services on situations and trends in manpower supply and demand in the formal labour market have also gained in regularity and quality of presentation in many developing countries, though there are also cases where due to economic adversities such labour market reporting has deteriorated.

It should be noted that improvements pertain primarily to the overall picture of the volume and deployment of national human resources. In fact, the observation has been made that at the macro level labour market information in many developing countries has become quite adequate to portray the basic features of the national labour market and to serve as decision-making input for broad national policy-making in the manpower and employment fields.

Finally, the ILO programme for the upgrading of labour market information capacity in developing countries has itself provided a privileged observation post for assessing progress. For instance, in comparing the national reports prepared for earlier subregional and regional workshops and seminars and those submitted to the more recent ones, it can be readily concluded that reporting has become more diversified and substantiated by facts and data, that analysis has deepened and moved from broad aggregate indicators to more micro-oriented information, that main issues and priorities are better articulated and that quality of presentation, in general, has gained substantially. Moreover, earlier labour market reports were mainly the product of employment services or their labour market information units, while more recent documents are including contributions from other labour market information producers, notably planning agencies, central statistical offices and employers' and workers' organisations.

The most important fact to note, however, is the emergence of a greater awareness of the usefulness of labour market information for decision-making on the part of the main actors in the manpower and employment policy fields. Since awareness is a prerequisite for soliciting the necessary support for establishing and running an effective labour market information programme, this merits some special attention.

B. Growing awareness of the importance of LMI

Good labour market information obviously depends to a large extent on the quantity and quality of the resources allocated to it. These, in turn, are only likely to be forthcoming in adequate proportions if the information produced serves a useful purpose, as demonstrated by an active demand for it. In other words, awareness and recognition of the importance of labour market information and commitment to allocate the necessary resources to generate it have a close cause-and-effect relationship.

It can be said generally that about ten years ago such awareness was practically non-existent in many developing countries. Thus, the first two subregional workshops on labour market information held under the ILO programme in Indonesia and India in 1978 and 1979 respectively made the point strongly that "only after this awareness has been created will it be possible for obtaining an effective labour market information programme".[2]

The participants at the workshops suggested a number of ways through which such awareness could be activated. These included the organisation of a planned and concerted educational programme and the holding of international conferences and seminars. It was also felt that such a promotional campaign should be directed at a whole range of individuals, agencies and organisations extending from policy-makers and planners, employers' and workers' organisations to the public at large.

In comparing the reports of these earlier workshops with those of later national, subregional and regional seminars on labour market information, it can readily be seen that in the meantime progress had been made towards a wider recognition of the need to improve labour market information programmes. An observer of the African scene noted that these seminars have had a "positive impact both in increasing the awareness of concerned parties about the urgent need for and importance of a well-organised labour market information system and in promoting some specific actions".[3] Similarly, a follow-up report on the Asian regional seminar in 1984 in four selected Asian countries observed that "awareness of the significant role of labour market information for manpower and employment policy-making is well established".[4] One of the more visible expressions of this increased awareness may be seen in the fact that the level of participants in subsequent workshops and seminars conducted under the ILO programme for upgrading labour market reporting in developing countries moved progressively from the technical category to the decision-making echelons.

Full awareness of the importance of labour market information is lastly a function of the use which the various labour market actors can make of it. Improved labour market reporting is bound to step up interest on the part of users. For instance, it can be observed that those labour market reports which offer little more than a compilation of employment services statistics, are issued with considerable delays, give little substance for decision-making purposes and are presented in a dull and unattractive form remain in stock in great numbers, though they may be free of charge. In contrast, labour market information reports and surveys which cover critical manpower and employment issues in an informative and attractive manner, explore ways and means of coming to grips with them and facilitate monitoring of remedial action taken are often quickly out of print, although quite often a handsome price is attached to them.[5]

C. Progress in specific directions and areas of LMI

While in the preceding pages an attempt was made to assess progress in labour market information activities in developing countries in rather broad terms, this needs supplementing by an examination of the more specific features and aspects of this process.

Confronted with mounting pressure for more diversified and purposeful labour market information in the face of persisting constraints in resources, many developing countries have recently taken a close look at their existing labour market information mechanism in order to pinpoint those areas where improvements are most urgently called for. Increasingly, main producers and consumers of LMI have been associated more actively with such exercises—either ad hoc or through more permanent institutional, co-ordinating structures such as manpower councils, advisory committees, working parties, task forces and the like. These had varying mandates and compositions, but with employers' and workers' organisations as titular members and in an advisory capacity in most cases.

It is true that in the majority of cases these co-ordinating bodies have lacked regular and continuous working arrangements and have not produced specific plans for detailed joint action programmes for upgrading national labour market capacity. However, they have provided an opportunity to the various consumers to take an initial stand regarding their needs and priorities vis-à-vis those responsible for the generation of labour market information. The first steps towards effective user-producer collaboration may be taken in this way. Tripartite national labour market information seminars have proved to be important catalysts for initiating action along these lines. In these joint meetings employers' organisations, on the whole, have shown that they have the means and the capacity to make good use of whatever labour market information is available. This applies to their decision-making processes regarding their own policy formation, as well as their position on matters of public manpower and employment policies and industrial relations. Nevertheless, employers feel that greater efforts are necessary. Their representatives at regional and sub-regional workshops and seminars on labour market information have stated spontaneously that these forums have sensitised and activated their work and have furthered their plans to improve their ability to benefit from and contribute to national labour market information programmes. Workers' organisations, on the other hand, have proved to be of lesser strength with regard to labour market analysis. They attributed this primarily to the lack of adequate resources in terms of both personnel and finance. However, the participation of workers' representatives in the international workshops and seminars mentioned did in some instances stimulate immediate action in terms of the preparation of reports on labour market issues of special concern to workers' organisations. However, it is quite obvious that more needs to be done to widen and maintain the momentum generated by these events.

While these new emphases on labour market information were taking place, conventional manpower assessment and planning and their associated data were still holding on in many developing countries. Nevertheless, within the framework of these activities, attention towards making more use of and strengthening labour market signalling has been on the increase. (Labour market signals are to be understood as the most recent indicators of changes in the labour market; they convey warnings of important new developments or confirm trends previously observed, and they are mainly regional and local in scope.) Evidence of this is derived from a comparison of the national reports prepared for earlier and subsequent international seminars and workshops on labour market information. Labour market signalling, barely mentioned in the first generation of reports, became a major point of interest and discussion, in conjunction with the new policy reorientations already referred to, notably those towards the promotion of fuller employment, greater income equality and the elimination of poverty. These policies have specific groups, regions and localities as their targets. Identification of their particular manpower and employment problems and of suitable ways and means of dealing with them necessitates the regular flow of disaggregate labour market information of the signalling type in the first place.

Faced with the inadequacy of existing labour market information sources for these purposes, especially from the points of view of required disaggregation, timeliness and cost considerations, many developing countries have embarked on a search for supplementary sources of labour market information. Several approaches have been experimented with—all of them substantially concerned with enhancing the signalling ability of national LMI mechanisms. They will be discussed at a later stage of this volume.

At the international level the wider acceptance and application of the concept of labour market signalling in LMI activities have been instrumental in the more recent discussions of a new orientation in one of the instruments of human resources development planning and policies—the assessment of training needs—in developing countries. Disenchantment with conventional manpower planning as an aid in such assessments has led an increasing number of developing countries to seek to "amplify signals on job requirements with a view to a better assessment of training needs, the continuous evaluation of training efforts and the introduction of the necessary mechanisms to improve the cost-effectiveness of the whole process".[6] Basic preconditions for the effective use of labour market signalling in the assessment of training needs have been identified as the abandoning of the previously practised one-off type of survey. This needs to give way to a regular information flow, the establishment of a close working partnership between manpower and vocational training planners and the formulation of and adherence to an annual "routine" programme in which responsibilities and tasks are clearly delineated.[7]

This approach entails far-reaching implications. A constant flow of labour market signals helps training authorities to adjust programmes and courses more readily to changing labour market demand. It also makes it possible to keep constantly under review whatever long-term manpower projections have been made and to modify them in the light of short-term labour market developments. At the same time, longer-term projections would become less necessary. The latter would retain their importance for plotting future demand for skills with long gestation periods and those needs derived from density norms, in addition to investigating manpower demand patterns likely to arise from different future employment scenarios. Longer-term manpower projections and labour market signalling would thus become parts of an interdependent and continuous process of "rolling adjustment".

This rapid overview of the development and progress of labour market information which have taken place in developing countries during the past ten years or so has shown a number of encouraging features. Awareness of the actual and potential significance of labour market information for decision-making in the broad fields of manpower and employment policies has increased and is fairly well established in many countries. Efforts to relate labour market information to essential and changing policy needs and, in general, user requirements have diversified and intensified, with employers' and workers' organisations being more closely involved. Labour market signalling, associated with the search for supplementary data sources, has found more widespread recognition and application in response to the felt inadequacies of traditional manpower assessment and planning activities and the emergence of new data requirements. As a result, labour market information has gained in both quantity and quality.

Nevertheless, progress has been rather uneven. A number of problems and constraints, although fully recognised, have defied early and easy solutions. The crux of the matter is that these constraints are running through the whole fabric of manpower and employment information. A fresh look at these unresolved problems—for which the inter-regional seminar provided a needed and welcome opportunity—will be the subject of the next chapter.

Notes

[1] ILO: *Year Book of Labour Statistics* (Geneva), 1976 and 1984.

[2] Jones, op. cit., p. 58.

[3] S. Nigam: *Report on a follow-up mission to the Seminar on Labour Market Information held in Nairobi in 1983* (Ethiopia, Kenya, Somalia and Zimbabwe), Technical Study No. 2, ILO Inter-regional Seminar on Upgrading Labour Market Information Reporting Systems in Developing Countries, Copenhagen, 29 September–3 October 1986 (Geneva, May 1986; mimeographed), p. 6.

[4] L. Richter: *Report on a follow-up mission to the Seminar on Labour Market Information held in Bangkok in 1984* (India, Thailand, Malaysia and Indonesia), Technical Study No. 1, ILO Inter-Regional Seminar on Upgrading Labour Market Information Reporting Systems in Developing Countries, Copenhagen, 29 September–3 October 1986 (Geneva, April 1986; mimeographed), p. 22.

[5] Ministry of Labour, Malaysia: *Labour and Manpower Report 1983/84* (Kuala Lumpur, Research and Planning Division, Ministry of Labour, 1985).

[6] ILO: *World Labour Report 2* (Geneva, 1985), p. 90.

[7] L. Richter: *Training needs: Assessment and monitoring* (Geneva, ILO, 1986).

Chapter 3

Main unresolved problems

A. Inadequate producer-user relationships

No regional, subregional or national labour market information seminar or workshop has gone by without strong suggestions and even exhortations about the urgent need for improving collaboration and co-ordination of main users and producers of labour market information. As already mentioned, some progress has been made in some developing countries in this direction, but the overall picture is still one of lip-service being paid but little substantive and sustained action being taken.

Closer user-producer collaboration has been said to be mainly a function of the credibility and usefulness of the labour market information actually delivered. Since the latter leave much to be desired in most developing countries, the result is a poor—and sometimes even non-existent—producer-user relationship. Departmental rivalries, professional compartmentalisation, real or presumed differentiation in competence between those co-ordinating and those to be co-ordinated and the extra workload involved in co-ordination—all these are additional odds which are weighing heavily against the setting up of well-functioning co-ordination mechanisms between user and producer.

It is for these reasons that it has been argued that effective collaboration could not be expected to be established unless overall responsibility for such co-ordination and collaboration is vested in a hierarchically well-placed government agency with statutorily assigned responsibilities. At this juncture, however, opinion becomes divided. One school of thought would like to see ministries of planning as the co-ordinating agency, while another prefers the ministry of labour or manpower in this role. A few voices opt for the central statistical services. It is thus hardly surprising that each developing country has pursued a different path to come to grips with this problem—though no single formula has emerged which has shown to be clearly superior over the others.

The question arises as to what could be done in addition or differently to what has been attempted in the past to bring about and sustain effective user-producer collaboration. Perhaps "more of the same" might be the most realistic answer. On the other hand, there are some useful pointers provided by the discussions of the regional seminars and the inter-regional seminar. For the preparation of the national reports on the current state and main issues of labour market information in the countries to be represented at these seminars, the organisers suggested that this reporting be undertaken by consultants with the active contribution and under the general direction of steering committees to be especially set up for this purpose. In practice, participation was confined to a small number of main users and producers, including in most cases representatives of employers' and workers' organisations. Since these committees were charged with carrying out a specific task during a given period, each member was committed to making a well-defined contribution. This, it seems, encouraged and ensured full collaboration.

It is interesting to ask what actually happened to the steering committees after the preparation of the country report. The disappointing answer is: not much. Not being assigned any new task, they fell into disuse. This seems to suggest strongly that in order to ensure continuity of co-ordinating work a catalytic agent—a *primus inter pares*—needs to be made available. The primary task of such a catalyst might not be to administer and to command, but to promote, encourage, advise, monitor, activate the flow of information and communication and generally help to gear the manifold activities in the labour market information field to a sort of "routine programme" or "drill".[1]

The starting-point of co-ordination work might differ. It might be the initiation of some sort of labour market information consumer research. This would be based on written or verbal feedback from main labour market information users about their needs, as articulated by them and not as perceived by LMI producers. The way of doing such research at various degrees of sophistication has been known for some time,[2] but practical application has not followed.

Another way of getting user-producer collaboration off the ground is the elaboration of a labour market information framework or model. Such a model defines the objectives of the labour market information programme in question, sets out its inputs and outputs and outlines the activities to be pursued to attain the objectives. In those countries where a fairly widespread network of employment services exists, the potential labour market information capacity of these agencies could well provide the focal point around which a gradually expanding national labour market information programme could be built.[3]

Making such a model work is not an easy task, however. Experience has shown that the first step to be taken, namely the reorientation of the employment service away from mainly administrative reporting of service activities to purposeful labour market information generation and analysis, is fraught with difficulties. Lack of adequate skills, especially at medium technical levels, is one problem, as will be discussed in greater detail later. Another one is the grounding of existing reporting procedures in administrative regulations and hierarchical structures which take time to change. Both constraints set narrow limits to the speed with which the labour market information function of employment services could be upgraded so that it will be able to assume the focal role of the overall national effort in promoting labour market information capacity.[4] Since everywhere employment or manpower services are both important producers and users of labour market information, overcoming the above-mentioned constraints is crucial.

B. Underuse of existing sources of LMI

Closely associated with the stubborn problem of defective producer-user collaboration and its deleterious effects on the usefulness of the data produced is the equally obstinate problem of the underuse of existing data on manpower and employment, whether they are published or unpublished. As has been pointed out earlier, the labour market information capacity in many developing countries has considerably improved during the past decade. However, it is difficult to say that this improvement has been obtained by a vastly improved use of existing labour market information data. Otherwise, there would not have been the frequent emphasis in the debates of recent labour market information seminars on the need to make fuller use of available information sources.

The various possibilities of making fuller use of existing sources of labour market information have been identified and amply discussed. The more important suggestions concern, in particular: the arrangements for better access to raw data files and the greater disaggregation of labour force and other household surveys; the working out of different cross-tabulations, re-aggregations and multivariate analysis; the more determined tapping of government records and files concerning use and development of personnel and, in particular, of employment levels, earnings and carrier patterns in the public sector; the addition to existing surveys of more questions relevant to manpower and employment; and the more purposeful design and use of the increasing number of special and ad hoc surveys and studies undertaken in many developing countries. The list of possibilities is long, the one of those having been turned into practice much shorter. The unresolved and inter-related problems of improving the skills of the staff engaged in labour market information and of administrative reforms to focus activities on the generation of more purposeful labour market information have defied more rapid progress.[5]

It was mentioned earlier that the number of special manpower and labour market surveys has notably increased in many developing countries over the recent past, with or without international assistance. However, the potential usefulness of these surveys for providing information of decision-making relevance has seldom been fully exploited. First of all, the majority of these surveys have been conceived without a clear idea about the specific purpose they could serve for policy- and decision-making. Though often of academic excellence, their practical value has been largely limited to providing background information. Though their authors often claim that survey findings are "interesting" and "useful", the reader is largely left with guessing in what respect. Moreover, most of these studies turned out to be one-off exercises with no follow-up.[6] This necessarily limited their value, for policy monitoring.

A fuller use of existing sources of labour market information included the addition of questions to established survey schedules. However, this is not as easily achieved as it sounds. Information users who wish to have additional items of information accommodated in such surveys need to argue their case strongly to obtain a positive reaction on the part of producers. Resources constraints will often tip the scales against such widening of the scope (and the work and expenses involved) of existing surveys.

Another way of exploiting more fully existing data sources is the merging of existing data files. The development of social accounting matrices for labour market relevance is a good example of the possibilities of linking existing demographic data, household data files and national income accounting data files in a framework of data presentation which helps to understand the functioning of the national labour market and formulate realistic employment policies.[7] Such a framework with fairly complete entry coverage does, of course, require considerable household survey capability. However, even under less favourable conditions there are even possibilities for constructing labour force matrices (cross-tabulations by sector/occupation, sector/status and the like) in a meaningful way. For instance, a basic labour force matrix was developed in Pakistan in 1985 making use of joint probabilities of available cross-tabulations (from published survey results) and the RAS method.[8]

The usefulness of these matrices consists of providing a framework for sampling and for labour market analysis and monitoring in the short run. This permits, in particular, the identification in the position of specific target groups in the labour force and their main characteristics, to be identified in a quick, focused and relevant manner as a basis for policy decisions. Moreover, the availability of labour force matrices over the years makes it possible to analyse structural changes in the labour force and help to formulate and monitor manpower plans.

Finally, fuller exploitation of existing data sources encounters a number of incidental obstacles. The quality of available data is often seriously impaired by weak survey design, low response rates to questionnaires, faulty sampling, poorly phrased and wrong or irrelevant questions, insufficiently instructed survey personnel. Other shortcomings are frequently changed definitions and concepts applied to the same survey or the use of different definitions in different surveys undertaken by different data producers, but relating to the same subject of investigation. The general area of wage surveys is a well-known example in the latter respect. In many developing countries substantial improvements in all the above fields are called for to enhance the potential usefulness of existing sources of labour market information.

C. The information gap in the informal sector

Pleas for generating more and better manpower and employment information about the informal sector, both in urban and in rural areas, have been persistently made since this term was coined and gained currency more than 15 years ago. These have remained as strong as they were during the early days of informal sector concern—an indication that not much has happened in this time span to improve the situation.

It is true that many studies and surveys have been undertaken to define, describe and investigate the main economic and social characteristics of this sector. However, most of them have paid little, if any, attention to identifying the specific manpower and employment issues faced by the informal sector. In addition—and not unusually—they have lacked follow-up. What has become known through these surveys is a general appreciation of the absorption capacity of the informal sector for excess manpower, with easy entry and exit possibilities, and of its potential significance as generator of skills and enterprise. However, with regard to the specific ways in which the sector gives evidence of possessing these qualities and as to how these could be developed and supported by specific policies, programmes and measures, these surveys have seldom moved beyond statements of the obvious. Some of the more severe critics have even described their conclusions as "banal and unilluminating".[9]

Nevertheless, past survey work has clearly demonstrated that manpower and employment information gathering in the informal sector poses special problems and difficulties in addition to those encountered by generation of convential labour market data. The first problem is that the informal sector still lacks a universally accepted definition and that controversy about it is still lingering. Secondly, the term labour market information, even if applied in its widest sense, has a different connotation in the informal sector than it has in the formal one. This has a bearing on data collection methods and analysis.

The general picture that has emerged of the informal sector is its composition of a myriad of self-employment activities and opportunities taken up "with great vitality, considerable technological development and every sign of responsive and adaptable growth".[10] These activities and opportunities exist in considerable variety and variability—with different regional and local composition, problems and successes, with different seasonal intensity, in different combinations, with different skill requirements and modes of meeting them, with different demands on enterprise and managerial ability and with different problems regarding capital equipment, production and marketing and with (real or perceived) difficulties of a legal, administrative and fiscal nature. In other words, the informal sector is an agglomeration of heterogeneous units and problems which escapes clear-cut definition. This makes it difficult to delineate areas of uniformity and common promotional policies. Likewise, manpower and employment issues of the informal sector are equally complex and do not fit easily into conventional modes of labour market information reporting and analysis.

Nevertheless, recent attempts have succeeded in squeezing out at least some manpower- and employment-related information about the informal sector from existing censuses and household surveys. While censuses have not offered much insight since they often do not make it possible to arrive at an acceptable approximation based on occupational categories, household surveys have fared somewhat better in these attempts. With certain assumptions and corrections, differentiating between employers and wage earners, self-employed workers and family workers and the self-employed in the formal sector, these manipulations with selected household surveys have attained a first approximation of the level of employment in the urban informal sector.[11]

The large number of special surveys of the informal sector have also unearthed some pieces of information relating to the overall manpower and employment situation in this sector. However, they do not portray a dynamic picture of rising and declining employment opportunities in the different segments of the informal sector and thus the kind of information pertinent to the preparation of concrete policy measures.[12]

Renewed interest in the informal sector, as a potential employment generator to compensate for the dwindling capacity of the formal sector, has been on the rise in crisis-ridden developing countries. In parallel, calls for more and better labour market information in this sector have become more insistent and also more articulate. Primary emphasis is placed, in this respect, on gathering information which throws more light on the dynamics of the informal sector and on the question of growth potential for the different components or subsectors. "The problems and opportunities of family-based enterprises with unpaid family workers, small firms employing wage-earners, domestic outworkers and low-paid wage earners are different and it does not help to mix them up."[13]

Accordingly, the suggestion has been made to pay greater attention to sector- or branch-specific studies which, in addition to the informal sector units in a particular economic activity, cover all types of enterprises in that activity to permit a meaningful analysis of the relations between them. Moreover, it has been proposed to exploit more systematically other potential sources of information such as licence records of municipalities, social security statistics, records of public and private organisations involved in promoting and assisting the informal sector and associations or groups formed by the "micro-entrepreneurs" themselves. In addition, it has been pointed out that the key informants approach might well be made use of in this respect so that strategically placed, well-informed persons are approached to share their knowledge on particular manpower and employment issues in the different informal subsectors. Finally, there have been pleas for the statistical services to assume a more active role in the generation of information on employment and incomes in the informal sector.[14]

It should be pointed out that all the preceding discussions referred primarily to the urban informal sector (UIS) in developing countries, on which discussions during the inter-regional seminar have concentrated. There is no doubt, however, that the manpower and employment information gap in the rural informal sector is even more critical than in the UIS. All suggestions made for improving the situation regarding the availability of manpower and employment information in the urban informal sector therefore apply with even greater force to the rural sector.

D. The question of methodology

It has been observed that concern with improving labour market information capacity in developing countries has been more forcefully driven by methodological considerations and preoccupations than by substantive policy requirements.[15] There is undoubtedly some truth in this contention, though its relevance would appear to be a matter of the past rather than the present.

Nevertheless, it is a fact that the question of methodology in both manpower and employment planning (which in their essentials depart from the same basis) has taken the limelight in the international debate over the past 20 years or so. Naturally, this influenced the direction and the priority which were given to the efforts to procure data and to methodological developments. Conversely, it has been argued that the kind of data readily available had some influence on the methodology of manpower planning which was developed, as well as on its weaknesses.

In the past few years the methodology debate seems to have lost its earlier intensity, but a consensus on what methodology to apply has not emerged—either on the part of the "theorists" or on that of the "practitioners". The story is too well known and documented to be repeated here. However, a few summary remarks relevant to the subject of this monograph seem to be in order.

There now exists a large array of different manpower planning methods ranging from the (predominant) manpower requirements approach, the rate-of-return analysis, normative methods, employer surveys and the international comparison method to econometric and input-output models. Each is characterised by different concepts, fields of application, different advantages and disadvantages and varying data requirements.[16] Most of them attempt to project current employment situations into the future on the basis of a number of assumptions about the behaviour of the various parameters which influence future levels and patterns of employment. These projections are meant to provide guide-lines for policy in terms of new job places required or skilled manpower needed over plan periods.

The adherents of projections claim that forward-looking policy-making cannot do without them and that their accuracy, reliability and usefulness could be enhanced if only the necessary data base could be provided or improved to the degree of quantity and quality required.

Critics of projection work argue that these projections have shown to be of little, if any, value for policy-making since the assumptions on which they are based are too tenuous to permit accurate predictions. Moreover, to the extent that labour markets are flexible they are not necessary. Thus, the insights gained from projections are limited. The application of density norms and projections for scenario building, as a tool for alternative policy analysis, have, however, escaped the outright condemnation of these critics.

A voluminous literature exists on this methodology debate of which the most recent publications are referred to in the bibliography to this publication.[17] What is of primary interest here is the fact that past over-concern with methodology has lessened in recent years. Nevertheless, entrenched methods such as the manpower requirements approach seem to keep their intuitive appeal and their popularity with many policy-makers and planners in developing countries.[18] Practical experience lends little justification for this, however.

First of all, all methodologies have shown to be subject to strong reservations. No one on its own has produced the goods that it was expected to deliver.

Secondly, there is no *a priori* reason to choose one method over another. The economic, social and political structure, levels and conditions of life and work vary considerably between different developing countries, as do sets of policy objectives and the relative weight attached to each objective. Given this diversity of background and taking into account the limitations of projection work, in general, and of the relative advantages and disadvantages of the different methods, in particular, a pluralistic approach would in any case appear to be preferable over the choice of one single method.

Thirdly, focusing manpower and employment planning work on methodology has been shown to stunt the development of alternative instruments and modes of manpower and employment planning for policy-making. It further has tended to divert attention from considering the wide range of supplementary or alternative tools for making full use of existing data sources, as well as the development of new sources of information.

ILO technical co-operation projects in manpower planning—still in fairly high demand—have tried to take account of these insights in their work. As a result, project results have become more usable and less prone to criticism. For example, many projects now undertake alternative projections which demonstrate to planners and decision-makers the manpower and employment implications of different scenarios rather than to present single-figure forecasts, as in the past. At the same time, the time horizons viewed have become shortened, projections are supplemented by much more labour market analysis to identify key issues and appropriate remedial policies. Finally particular efforts are made to embed the manpower and employment planning exercise in the overall socio-economic development framework rather than to be added on later as an adjunct.[19]

In short, while it cannot be said that the debate on methodology in manpower and employment planning has been completely laid to rest, the role of formal manpower planning with its heavy armour of methodology is becoming less pre-eminent. This has been accompanied by a greater propensity to develop and apply more in-depth labour market analysis. In spite of these developments, however, manpower forecasting and projection work and, in particular, the application of the manpower requirements approach will probably linger on for the simple reason that the urge to look into the future and to come up with "some figures" is not likely to vanish. It is therefore not really surprising that the advent of planning for manpower modelling with the help of computers has in some developing countries kindled a sort of "renaissance" of manpower planning of the more conventional style. But even in these cases some doubts are arising over the trade-offs between costs and the practical usefulness of this work. Massive data requirements to overcome problems of aggregation and the fragility of the structure of the models are exerting sobering influences even on the more entrenched advocates of manpower and employment forecasting methods and models.

It may be said in conclusion that manpower and employment planning work of recent years has come to combine more frequently conventional methodology and labour market analysis. However, a balanced way of doing this in a complementary and mutually reinforcing way is slow in emerging. This has taken place alongside the emergence of new claims and demands exerted on labour market information capacity by new developments in socio-economic background and policy setting in the majority of developing countries. A brief discussion of these developments and their implications for labour market information programmes and activities will be the subject of the next chapter.

Notes

¹ C. Dougherty: "Manpower development planning from three points of view: Country, technical assistance agency and lending agency", in World Bank: *Manpower issues in educational investment—A consideration of planning processes and techniques*, World Bank Staff Working Paper No. 624 (Washington, DC, 1983).

² *Consumer research for labour market information programmes*, Paper prepared by W. Mason for the Second Sub-Regional Workshop on Labour Market Information, New Delhi, 5–9 March 1979.

³ W. Mason: *A labour market information model*, Working paper prepared under the UNDP/ILO Project of Indonesian Manpower Management Information System (IMMIS) Jakarta, 1986.

⁴ The most recent discussion of the role of employment services in labour market information in selected developed and developing countries is contained in ILO/Federal Institute of Employment of the Federal Republic of Germany: *Record of Proceedings of the International Symposium on the Role and Organisation of Employment Services*, Nuremberg, 14–17 October 1986 (Geneva, 1987; doc. D.3/1986), pp. 55–57.

⁵ L. Richter: *The raison d'être and the repertoire of new approaches to manpower planning—Some reflections and notes*, Paper prepared for a Seminar on New Approaches to Manpower Analysis and Planning and Their Relevance to Indonesia, Jakarta, 1986, p. 13.

⁶ C. Dougherty: *Labour market studies and manpower development planning* (London, London School of Economics, June 1983), p. 35.

⁷ C. Grootaert: *The labour market and social accounting: A framework of data presentation*, LMS Working Paper No. 17 (Washington, DC, World Bank, 1982).

⁸ S. Cohen: *Labour analysis and manpower planning*, Paper prepared for a Seminar on New Approaches to Manpower Analysis and Planning and their Relevance to Indonesia, Jakarta, 1986, p. 27.

⁹ M. Godfrey: *Data sources and significance of information on employment in the urban informal sector*, Paper prepared for an ARPLA Inter-Country Symposium on Labour Market Information Functions of Labour Administration, Denpasar, Indonesia, 11–20 August 1986, p. 5.

¹⁰ M. Bienefeld and M. Godfrey: "The informal sector", in C. Hongladarom (ed.): *Proceedings of an International Seminar on World Structural Change and its Impact on ASEAN's Employment and Manpower* (Bangkok, Human Resources Institute, Thammasat University, 1985), p. 189.

¹¹ E. Klein: *The urban informal sector and labour market information systems*, Paper prepared for the Inter-regional Seminar on Upgrading Labour Market Information Reporting Systems in Developing Countries, Copenhagen, 13–17 October 1986.

¹² H. Haan: *The urban informal sector in developing countries and the collection and analysis of labour market information—Issues and priorities*, Paper prepared for the Inter-regional Seminar on Upgrading Labour Market Information Reporting Systems in Developing Countries, Copenhagen, 13–17 October 1986.

¹³ Godfrey, op. cit., p. 6.

¹⁴ Haan, op. cit., p. vii.

¹⁵ T. Kelly: *Labour slack, uncertainty, manpower planning and labour market information*, Project Working Paper INS/82/013 (Jakarta, ILO, 1986), p. 1.

¹⁶ An overview of these various methods and approaches is given in Richter: *Training needs . . .* , op. cit., pp. 31–38. See also R. V. Youdi and K. Hinchliffe (eds.): *Forecasting skilled manpower needs—The experience of eleven countries* Paris, UNESCO, International Institute for Educational Planning, 1985.

¹⁷ M. Godfrey: *Planning for education, training and employment in Indonesia* , Summary Report, UNDP/ILO, "Implementation of an employment creation strategy " (Jakarta, Mar. 1987), Ch. 1, "The controversy over the manpower requirements approach to human resources development planning";

G. Psacharopoulos and R. Hinchliffe : "From planning techniques to planning process", in World Bank: *Manpower issues in educational investment—A consideration of planning processes and techniques,* World Bank Staff Working Paper No. 624 (Washington, DC, 1983); and R. Amjad: *ARTEP's experience in short- and medium-term employment planning,* Paper prepared for the Inter-regional Seminar on Upgrading Labour Market Information Reporting Systems in Developing Countries, Copenhagen 13–17 October 1986.

[18] Godfrey, op. cit., p. 1.

[19] F. Lisk: *Labour market information and employment policy: Issues and priorities for action,* Paper prepared for the Inter-regional Seminar on Upgrading Labour Market Information Reporting Systems in Developing Countries, Copenhagen, 13–17 October 1986, p. 5.

Chapter 4

New issues and approaches in labour market information

A. Economic retrenchment and structural adjustment

The continuing economic downturn and the increasing balance-of-payments difficulties experienced by the majority of developing countries have exacerbated the endemic employment problem which for many years has been a major preoccupation and a most intractable issue and object of economic and social policy. These adversities have confronted developing countries with hard choices in setting and pursuing appropriate policy objectives. Very often, the actual policies adopted have turned out to affect negatively both the rate of economic growth and employment levels. In many cases, the structural adjustment policies designed primarily to resume economic growth have diverted attention and drawn resources away from employment promotion; they have also led to sizeable employment contractions, particularly in the public sector.

Apart from these directly induced reductions in employment levels, the "trickle down" impacts and implications of slower growth and adjustment on manpower and employment in different sectors, occupations and areas of a country have proved difficult to assess. Whatever information has been put forward in this regard and, more generally in terms of the social effects and hardships involved, have been largely of a conjectural nature. There is no lack of statements such as "it has been generally acknowledged that structural adjustment usually entails reduced incomes of the poor, increased unemployment . . . " and that different adjustment measures "may dislocate workers which are heavily reliant on imported materials", "may affect the smaller enterprises and the poor farmers more than the larger units", "might impoverish large numbers of cash-crop growers",[1] and so on.

As useful as these calls of Cassandra are for drawing attention to potentially serious problems, they are little more than statements of the obvious. They do not tell much about how and in what way specific adjustment measures may be "targeted" for and affect the different sectors and subsectors, the various occupational groups and the different areas and regions of a country. There is frequent reference to the most vulnerable parts of the population being the most likely candidates for having to bear the brunt of the impact of slower growth and adjustment policies. However, more often than not such judgements are based on very slender evidence, not to say guesswork.

The results of these information lacunae are that the basis on which remedial policies and measures are taken is fragile and that their impact is difficult to monitor. This situation of "grossly inadequate data" and "the lack of sufficient indicators" impeding the assessment of the direct effects and impact of stabilisation and adjustment programmes on poverty and the poor was highlighted by an informal ILO expert group meeting held in Geneva in 1986 to discuss these subjects. The group pleaded for increased efforts in relevant data collection and research.[2]

Similar considerations pertain to the broad issue of the impact of techno-logical changes on manpower and employment. In many respects, technological change interacts with structural adjustment problems. A quickening pace of techno-logical innovations in many fields of production has been compounding and has maybe even been one of the root causes of the economic difficulties encountered. The main employment issues and policy options involved in technological changes have been more fully documented and analysed.[3] Nevertheless, the regular monitoring of developments through a timely flow of relevant information also remains a largely unresolved problem.

On the other hand, few developing countries are completely devoid of any information on these matters. However, the sources from which such information could be obtained are often ill-exploited or go largely unnoticed. Examples can be given where the determined and systematic scanning of all accessible sources of information, combined with analytical ability and imagination, have made it possible to arrive at a fairly clear identification of principal issues and to outline the possible nature and scope of remedial action which might be taken to deal with these issues. A recent study of the training implications of technological changes in manufacturing in India underlines this point strongly.[4]

On the whole, however, it must be concluded that substantial improvements of the existing data base are called for in order to assess more purposefully the manpower and employment implications of structural adjustment needs and policies. In this context, asking the right questions needs equal attention. Also, the time-lag between the occurrence of the impacts of various manpower and employment policies and measures in the fields of structural adjustment and technological change and their reporting has to be shortened to the absolute minimum. All this would involve more work in labour market signalling. In other words, there is an increasing demand for quick response.

Perhaps with hindsight, but also with some logic, it has been argued that if only the more obvious manpower and employment implications of the recent economic downturn and structural adjustment policies could have been signalled more clearly at an earlier stage of the process, it would have been possible to curb or to counterbalance at least some of the undesirable developments in the manpower and employment fields before they had run their full course. In many cases, however, the opposite has occurred. Negative impacts on employment levels have reached pro-portions which are now difficult to handle on top of the many other constraints which continue to beset employment policies in developing countries.

It is the structural nature and the long-term features of the employment problem which the current economic downturn with its pressures on the employment front has once again brought into sharp focus. However, the various implications are perhaps not fully understood. There is general evidence that recession and adjustment policies followed in many developing countries have made unemployment a more sensitive issue in relation to the chronic and all-pervasive problem of under-employment. This reflects, on the one hand, an inability to adjust aggregated demand and supply of manpower to changing economic fortunes and, on the other, shifts within and between labour markets in terms of levels of activity and employment in different sectors, public and private and formal and informal. The extent and consequences of these shifts, regarding not only levels and trends of employment and unemployment, but also wages, wage structure and wage differentials, and occupa-tional distribution, as well as emerging shortages and oversupplies of certain skill categories, need to be more fully understood and monitored. Without adequate information on situations and trends in these respects, there is no proper basis for the formulation of appropriate manpower and employment policies nor for their effective monitoring.[5]

It is to be emphasised that manpower and employment planning under conditions of economic downturn and structural adjustment also require, at a very broad level, more up-to-date macro-economic data to complement labour market information, if such planning is to be fully integrated into the overall socio-economic development planning process. In any case, economic retrenchment and adjustment policy have strengthened the arguments for such integration. "Policy-makers and administrators would need to know the general thrust and the specific nature of the consistency between adjustment and employment promotion, as well as the limits of such consistency, in order to formulate appropriate employment policies in a given context."[6]

B. Sectoral manpower and employment planning

In addition to the pressures exerted by adjustment policies, there has been another forceful push for labour market information of the signalling type brought about by an increasing concern with sectoral manpower and employment planning. This greater interest in sectoral—and at the same time shorter-term—manpower and employment planning with stepped-up analysis has several causes.

It has been common experience that though many national development plans stated employment promotion as their major objective, this did not always find concrete expression in the sectoral plans, programmes and projects. Or worse, sectoral programmes and the macro-level policy framework of the plan often showed glaring divergences. Inadequacy of the requisite assessment and planning data on sectoral employment situations and trends had a great deal to do with this frequently observed divergence.[7]

Secondly, the rather unstable and uncertain economic environment which the majority of developing countries have been facing over the past years has played havoc with the fulfilment of longer-term plan targets. These showed considerable deviations from the results and performance actually achieved. The fact that some sectors have fallen short of targets more seriously than others, with different employment and manpower impacts, has already been mentioned earlier. Moreover, different sectors moved into and out of the centre of attention, such as the energy sector a few years ago and the public sector recently.

With regard to the energy sector, many developing countries were severely hit by the energy crisis of some years ago and the majority of them embarked on comprehensive national energy development—and energy-saving—programmes. Considerable efforts were made, bolstered up by international and bilateral aid, to overcome bottle-necks in planning and implementing priority-oriented action and, in particular, in mobilising investment resources.

This initial concern with removing technical and financial constraints in developing energy resources tended to conceal another impeding factor of key significance. This became apparent when policies moved into the implementation stage: the shortfall of requisite skills for staffing development drives within the energy sector. Although of different degrees of severity, the problem pertained to practically all skill categories and to all subsectors and activities from exploration, production and organisation to distribution, including the preparation of legal proceedings and the negotiation of appropriate contracts with aid-giving and capital-investing organisations, institutions and enterprises. Needless to say, there were also glaring deficiencies in the national capacity to generate adequate background information and data to *(a)* underpin the often very ambitious national energy development efforts and *(b)* to make skilful use of existing information sources for analysis of relevance to decision-making.

These skill deficits became increasingly recognised. To overcome them more intensive manpower planning and assessment of training needs began to be initiated. However, it became quickly apparent that the limitations of conventional manpower planning approaches had even greater relevance in the energy sector because of its high degree of uncertainty and the particularly rapid changes in energy technologies. This prompted the development of a new approach combining projection work with analysis which included examination of existing patterns of manpower use, career paths of various skill groups and supply constraints due to malpractices in the energy sector. This approach placed the clearly identified supply and demand problems of the sector in the context of the working of the national labour market. In brief, the focus of manpower planning in the energy sector became increasingly directed at analysing and monitoring critical manpower bottle-necks against the background of prevailing patterns of manpower use and, on this basis, examining options for effective solutions.

This integrative and more analytical orientation of manpower planning in the energy sector implies, of course, considerably greater demands on data volume and quality. In fact, the establishment of longer-term capacity for manpower reporting and analysis in the energy sector was one of the three main supporting pillars which were considered indispensable for the working of the new approach.[8]

Another example of the stronger orientation of manpower planning towards sectors is provided by what happened in the public sector in many developing countries. Recession and adjustment policies have hit particularly hard the traditional role of this sector as a major provider of employment, especially for higher-level manpower categories. Manpower planning work in this sector, which in the past had been mainly concerned with assessing the manpower requirements of an expanding system of civil and public service, has now assumed the primary task of exploring ways and means of redeploying public sector manpower which has become redundant—or will become so—as a result of economy drives in public expenditure.

The pressure for finding instant solutions for this often sizeable problem has pushed many developing countries into hectic activities. These usually start with rather detailed surveys to document the exact nature and scope of the employment implications of the budgetary and public expenditure contractions and to seek alternative employment opportunities for those affected. It has become known that many of these stock-taking efforts have been frustrated by the absence of readily available data and information. Thus, their results have often been limited to either a set of recommendations for further in-depth surveys or to rather general proposals for promoting employment outlets in the productive sector of the economy, notably industry and agriculture, or in the informal sector.

It is in this adverse climate of prolonged economic contraction and uncertainty that development planning in many countries of the Third World has become increasingly oriented towards setting short-term priorities and targets at sectoral and subsectoral levels to be followed by close monitoring. This has meant the focusing of investment decisions and allocations at sectoral, subsectoral and project levels. Accordingly, manpower development issues are increasingly analysed together with those of manpower use and management. In other words, conventional manpower planning is turning into more regular manpower analysis which includes, as a significant element, the signalling of labour supply and demand situations, trends and, in particular, imbalances in different labour markets.[9]

Associated with this new emphasis on sectoral, subsectoral and project manpower planning, combined with more analysis, has been the gradual emergence of a new style of training needs assessment, as already briefly pointed out before in a different context. This is reflected in the setting of training priorities or training targets in preference to the conventional approach of working out manpower requirements in a predictive single-figure fashion. It also finds expression in a greater interest being attached to monitoring these targets or priorities so that necessary adjustments are identified at an early stage and can be made speedily in an incremental (or decremental) manner.

Main features of this approach are the adoption of range projections, compared with and adjusted to qualitative knowledge and insights obtained from selected key staff of public agencies, employers, workers and others familiar with the sector or subsector in question. The exercise is supplemented by an analysis of existing staffing patterns, manpower allocation systems or mechanisms, major manpower bottle-necks, replacement and expansion requirements, the likely impact of technological changes on the job content of different occupations or occupational groups and the existing and prospective flows in skill supply.

As might be expected, quick and full adoption of this approach has been troubled by a number of difficulties, notably data limitations. Wherever it was tried, it was accompanied by specific proposals to improve existing sources and flows of information on occupational supply and demand, including data on enrolment and output of training institutions.[10]

It will have become apparent that the new issues and approaches discussed in the foregoing imply demands on the nature and scope of labour market information different from those in the past. Analysis rather than projection work tends to determine data requirements. Of what kind these demands are and how they may be met will emerge more clearly from the following discussion of the main characteristics and underlying reasoning of what has come to be called a "new approach to manpower planning".[11]

C. New-style manpower planning: Labour market analysis

Labour market analysis is, of course, not a recent discovery. What is new about it is the increasing role which critics of the conventional manpower planning approach would like to see assigned to it at all stages of manpower and employment policy-making and implementation.

The arguments for labour market analysis do not take their point of departure solely from the disappointing experiences of manpower forecasting and projection activities of the conventional type. They were also particularly strengthened by the various efforts to identify and seek solutions to the new manpower and employment issues which have arisen as a result of the recent economic downturn, adjustment policies and an accelerating rate of technological change. The latter have plunged labour markets into constant turmoil. Capturing early signals about the onslaught of these turbulences and the underlying causes, as well as appropriate ways of dealing with them, has therefore become of ever-growing importance. This is well expressed in the recent statement that "knowledge of how labour markets function is integral to an understanding of the chief economic issues of our time".[12]

Such knowledge and understanding cannot, of course, rely on signalling alone. It also requires survey and analysis work which probes more deeply into medium- and longer-term indicators, their determining factors and inter-relationships. Moreover, labour market analysis needs to look into the decision-making practices of the various actors in the labour market, both regarding manpower supply and demand and to cast light on the influences facilitating or impeding their decision-making. Such influences are exerted not only by government regulations and legislative intervention in labour market transactions, collective bargaining, and so on, but also by social practices, incentives and constraints.[13] Furthermore, labour market analysis has to take a close look at the effectiveness of running manpower and employment policies and programmes, both for monitoring and the identification of better alternatives and options. This is essential for approximating policy and programme costs and benefits.

This wide spectrum of labour market analysis covers both the regular reporting of labour market transactions, i.e. the short-term interactions of labour supply and demand, as well as the identification of labour market processes, their dynamics and transitions, i.e. longer-term labour supply and demand relationships. The first is the predominant domain of labour market signalling. For many information users, especially for those with immediate decision-making and operational responsibilities primarily at local levels, signalling is a vital output of labour market information. The second is the realm of in-depth research. Since labour markets are characterised by hetereogeneity in many dimensions, "the key research issue appears to be how to represent this heterogeneity in models in which it has a logic in terms of labour market functioning".[14]

Both labour market signalling and labour market research have their role— and often a complementary one—to play. It is obvious that mere signalling cannot catch the more intricate causality and relationships of many labour market phenomena, while labour market research cannot contribute much to daily operational decision-making.

There is nothing to be gained from neglecting—or underestimating and belittling—either one. However, both have to stand the test of usefulness and—most important for developing countries—of cost-effectiveness. Labour market signalling, on the one hand, which has been the actual or potential responsibility of labour market information units of employment services, must rid itself of the still widespread (and justified) onus of producing mounds of data which are partial, unreliable, outdated and devoid of analysis. Labour market research, on the other hand, must make sure that its results are not only of academic interest but have relevance to policy- and decision-making and are actually used in these respects.[15] The specific purpose and application of labour market surveys and studies in terms of policy implications need to be clearly spelled out before they are undertaken. Carefully structured hypotheses may be a good starting-point for such surveys.

Integrating labour market signalling and research would be an important task of an effective user-producer collaboration set-up. This might in the first place define the respective roles and tasks of labour market signalling and research and help to bring about a mutually supporting interdependence. The closer involvement of universities and research institutes in labour market analysis would be an important step in this direction—a move which is still to come in most developing countires.

Because of the diversity and complexity of labour market analysis of this newer approach, its methods and techniques will also have to vary considerably. They will not only have to differ with respect to the specific manpower and employment issue in question and the time horizons considered. National, sectoral, occupational and local specificities will also have an influence on the types and tool of analysis applied. No uniform type or single method of analysis can therefore fit the criterion of universal applicability.

Nevertheless, there is an obvious need for a general, unifying framework or outline which facilitates purposeful direction, co-ordination and relevance of labour market analysis. At the national level, such a framework is necessary to identify and keep under review major national manpower and employment issues, to define inter-relationships, to establish priorities and to outline possibilities, alternatives or options for remedial policies, all viewed from the broad platform of the overall manpower and employment structure of a country.

First attempts have been made to construct such a framework and to analyse major manpower issues in this new style in a country context.[16] Although further practical experience and refinements are necessary, they show the directions in which the framework will have to be developed to constitute a solid basis for systematic analysis.

Such national frameworks, concerned with identifying and analysing the broader manpower and employment issues of a country, need to be supplemented by models suited for sectoral and subsectoral analyses. Such sectoral analysis frameworks are also in their infancy, although some pioneering work has been done for the energy sector, particularly for Asian countries. A proposed, but still largely experimental, framework consisting of ten steps (seven comprising the static part of the manpower requirements approach and the remaining three concerned with bringing labour market signals to bear on the projections of skills). These are supplemented by rate-of-return calculations to pinpoint promising directions of investment in training and formulating major conclusions and recommendations concerning possible solutions for overcoming manpower imbalances revealed by this exercise.[17]

While these "first generation" frameworks need further practical testing to make them proven tools of purposeful manpower analysis, they do already convey a clear message at this stage. This is the recognition that new-style manpower planning "is easy to advocate but will be very difficult to implement in practice".[18] One reason is that it is bound to imply harder and more imaginative work than conventional manpower planning, therefore placing high demands on the skills of the personnel engaged in it. Acuity of the analyst will be a foremost requirement in this job. Another is that its data requirements are certainly not smaller than those of conventional manpower planning.

While activation of existing manpower and employment information sources might help a great deal to meet some of the new needs for data, it seems unavoidable that somewhat new and somewhat less conventional sources of information need to be found. An overview of some of the more important attempts to develop such sources will be presented in the following section.

D. New sources of data

Though not meant to imply exclusiveness, three such new sources of data generation may be singled out as having received most attention, though in various degrees of intensity and of practical application. These are: tracer studies; selective labour turnover surveys; and key informants surveys. None of them is really a novelty, but their focus on labour market signalling and on casting light on labour market dynamics makes them particularly suitable instruments for new-style labour market analysis. While the first two sources are primarily relevant and applicable in the formal sector, the third has good potential for generation of manpower and employment information in both formal and informal sectors. In the latter case application seems to be particularly indicated in those instances where the labour market information base is very fragile or even non-existent.

Tracer studies have become increasingly popular as a means of measuring the performance of education and training institutions and courses through the labour market experience of their graduates/ex-trainees. At the same time, they are capable of casting light on labour market dynamics.[19]

The versatility of tracer studies is noteworthy. They also have potential for identifying technological changes and their effect on occupational skill patterns and for assessing the training required to adapt to them. Moreover, they have proved ability to signal shifts in demand, in general, so that relevant training programmes may be adjusted. And they have turned out to be useful in the assessment of the relative effectiveness of training programmes in their responsiveness to economic downturns. As has been pointed out earlier, such labour market signals have assumed primary significance in the contemporary scenario of economic retrenchment and employment contraction.

A potential danger area against which tracer studies have to guard is the design of questionnaires which are too voluminous. This has tended to affect negatively the quantity and quality of response, to lead to significant cost increases and cause delays in the availability of results. Focus and rigour to ensure policy relevance can also be affected with the result "that a very expensive exercise ultimately has negligible effects on decision-making".[20] Finally, tracer studies must be embedded in mechanisms which provide for regular follow-up and thus reveal changes and dynamics in labour market conditions of importance for training policies and programmes.

The second new source, *labour turnover surveys*, only deserves the attributive "new" if such surveys are of the kind as developed and applied in Malaysia.[21] Their main objective in that country is to capture regularly and quickly a set of essential labour market indicators which can help decision-makers, in particular those engaged in vocational training planning, to intervene promptly in labour markets. The core of the survey is the measurement of relative scarcity/abundance of workers in selected occupations (known to be of key importance for the economy) on a regular basis. This assessment is based on a limited sample and a short questionnaire asking for inflow and outflow data on resignations, engagements, vacancies and dismissals. Strong points of the survey are meant to be timeliness and cost-effectiveness, though its output is mainly of a qualitative nature indicating orders of magnitude and trends rather than precise and representative figures.

This qualitative feature of the survey has raised questions of trade-offs between the conflicting objectives of "timeliness and cost-effectiveness" and of "accuracy and statistical representativeness". There has been pressure to enlarge the sample (from 1,000 to 2,000 establishments). Its objective was to attain better representation and thus an improvement of the quantitative performance of the survey, relaxing somewhat the original objective of providing essentially qualitative information for signalling purposes. After some debate, a compromise was reached. The original sample size was doubled. On the other hand, reporting intervals were stretched from quarterly to half-yearly intervals, while the actual survey rhythm of three months was maintained. There are no indications as to whether and how this move towards greater accuracy of the survey has affected the original budget of the survey and its signalling mandate. However, the survey modifications may have satisfied those critics who have seen their reservations about accuracy heeded by the introduction of a new sample.

More generally, public opinion on the usefulness of the survey has been favourable. In addition, the fact that the survey was begun some eight years ago as an experiment and has now been institutionalised may be taken as an indication of its value as a labour market signalling device.

Another new source of manpower and employment information, the *key informants approach*, is based on the idea that there are persons who, as a result of their responsible positions (e.g. government officials, village elders, teachers, business people, extension agents, co-operative officials and bank managers), possess an informed view of the manpower and employment situation and trends in and around their area of residence or activity. Such knowledge could be tapped through structured interviews to form a meaningful mosaic.[22]

This approach was originally conceived of and developed as a practical and inexpensive device to fill the basic blanks in the map of manpower and employment date in the informal sector and, in particular, in the rural areas. However, it has also found application in the formal sector and in developed countries as well, especially as a means of supporting vocational training planning and programming. New Zealand runs a continuous and rotating programme of special sectoral and subsectoral studies of trends in skills to assist the relevant industries in planning their human resources. This gives evidence of the great potential of the key informants approach, the width of its applicability and its considerable possibilities with regard to degree of sophistication, but at the same time highlights the main conditions that have to be met to make satisfactory use of it. In the latter respect, the selection of suitable key informants, the designing of concise questionnaires with a few "core questions", the rapidity of survey execution and processing and the publication of short reports of relevance to decision-making are decisive prerequisites.[23]

Nevertheless, scepticism about this simple, relatively inexpensive and mainly qualitative supplementary source of labour market information still runs deep in many developing countries. Personal bias of key informants is one of the arguments fuelling this scepticism. Another is the qualitative nature of the information obtained through key informants. In fact, the approach has been dismissed in some cases on the grounds that "it would not permit estimates on a scientific and objective basis".[24] Moreover, a widespread feeling seems to be lingering in developing countries that resorting to the key informats approach carries the stigma of simplicity and is indicative of a particularly low stage of development.

The pros and cons of the key informants approach have been quite intensively discussed elsewhere. A special test programme conducted by the ILO under the labour market information upgrading programme in the late seventies and early eighties in ten developing countries concluded that the approach had proved to be suitable, relevant and feasible. The programme produced a detailed evaluation report as well as an operational manual. Decision-making material about adopting or not adopting the approach as a complementary source of labour market information is thus in ample supply.[25] In any case, key informant surveys are essentially a category of public opinion surveys. Their acceptance or rejection therefore depends on the views which are held by labour market producers of the usefulness of such surveys.

Whether or not the approach will be adopted in any particular country situation will ultimately depend on the relative strength of persuasion of the arguments put forward by supporters and critics. Of particular importance in this debate will be the question of what has been called "proportionate accuracy",[26] i.e. the degree of the precision of information required for various decision-making purposes. Practical experience has shown that in many areas of manpower and employment policy and promotion, orders of magnitude and direction of changes— the very pieces of information with which the key informants approach contents itself—provide sufficient indicators and signals for decision-making, though these need monitoring. In other words, a high degree of precision is often unnecessary. Where the contrary is claimed, this should be based on articulate and convincing arguments about specific policy relevance. It should be obvious that, here again, a close user-producer relationship would be an appropriate medium to settle this important question in everybody's interest.

With all this being said, it should be realised that the key informants technique has been tried in a relatively limited number of developing countries. Even in those its possibilities have not in all cases been fully explored.[27] Such exploration on an adequate scale and in an appropriate form is still to come for the urban informal sector, since practically all of the key informants surveys so far undertaken have primarily included the rural sector in their purview.

E. Computerisation of labour market information

Developments and progress in labour market information, as highlighted in this monograph, have one important trait in common: everywhere increasing claims are being made on volume and flow of information. Judging by the demands expressed by the five regional seminars and the inter-regional seminar, fulfilment of these claims will stretch existing capacities and the possibilities of improving them to the limits. These are set by the availability of resources in terms of finance and skilled personnel. The difficulties are compounded by the fact that new needs are arising against the background of underuse of existing data and the widespread backlog of unprocessed information. The latter gives rise to the inordinate delays with which many routine labour market reports and manpower and employment surveys and studies are often published. The speeding up of data processing and release is, therefore, of particular importance.

It is mainly for this reason that the introduction of electronic data processing facilities for labour market information has moved to a prominent place on the agenda of efforts at labour market improvement in many developing countries. A number of them have established these facilities under specific projects to build up comprehensive manpower management information systems or accelerate the handling of employment services data and placement, with improved labour market reporting and analysis pursued as a welcome byproduct. Furthermore, in most of the countries in which electronic data processing facilities are not available for labour market information, there is great interest in catching up as evidenced by detailed plans and, often, specific requests for international or bilateral aid in this respect.

The computerisation of manpower and employment information is bound to accelerate and widen labour market data processing and analysis and, inherently, to push for more organisational efficiency in information handling. On the other hand, the costs involved in such investment have proved to be a deterrent to a more rapid spread of this technology in the area of labour market information.

With the advent of new-generation computers and software development and, notably, the appearance of less expensive microcomputers, cost considerations have become less stringent. Microcomputers are likely to pay their way, particularly in those data operations where considerable data processing and manipulations are involved—labour market signalling and also projection work of the scenario-building type being cases in point. In the latter respect, experiments have recently been made in specific country contexts to test the possibilities and suitability of microcomputers for the application of a medium-term model designed to contribute to the further development of manpower forecasting methodology in developing countries. Such projections cover primarily population, education, labour supply, labour demand, unemployment and underemployment. The primary purpose of the model is to serve as a policy tool for the analysis of alternative strategies and of the impact of various educational policies on the labour market in developing countries. The model is the first phase of an ongoing project to use the latest microcomputer hardware and software for labour market analysis and for making the model as accessible and useful as possible to planners.[28]

First results of the project are considered encouraging. Its authors conclude that the project has demonstrated that the microcomputer is an "appropriate technology" for developing countries in employment planning. It is cheap, reliable and does not need specially trained operators. Primary benefits arise from better management, organisation and consistency checks of the various data used and from improved analysis of policy implications of the different scenarios constructed.

On the other hand, initial experience has also shown that "improvement and maintenance of the data base is an arduous, time-consuming task that has to be kept up on a day-by-day basis, and deficiencies in this area cannot be obviated with improved technology or better modelling".[29]

This statement underlines the importance of the existence of a reasonably developed basis of manpower and employment data generation as a decisive criterion for the introduction of computer facilities. Considerable strides have been made in many developing countries over the past few years towards fulfilling this condition. However, the majority still appear to be at a stage of development of their labour market information capacity where the costs and benefits to be expected have to be carefully weighed. An impressive array of questions have to be settled in this respect. These include the undertaking of feasibility studies, the definition of requirements, the choice of hardware and software, bidder analysis, the selection of computer personnel, the provision of adequate training, decisions on the kind and scope of data to be computerised, the installation of facilities and their running and maintenance, and the evaluation of the performance of the system.[30] Developing countries intending to avail themselves of computer facilities in labour market information might be well advised to study the experience of countries which have installed such capacity.[31]

A step-by-step approach starting modestly with the establishment of computer facilities for critical data-processing activities might be clearly preferable to an early all-out, large-scale effort. A gradual building up of computer installations tallies well with the fairly long time it takes to move a labour market information mechanism from bits and pieces to a systematic and well-functioning structure, capable of meeting essential needs of the various users.

Proceeding in a step-by-step manner and setting operational priorities constitutes a continuous problem which is posing itself to all developing countries, though with different scope, intensity, form and severity. The following chapter will add regional and national substance and meaning to this rather general statement. It also supplements the rather abstract discussions of the preceding chapters with the presentation of concrete examples of how different regions and countries have used and improved labour market information to address their problems.

Notes

[1] G. Edgren and M. Muqtada: *Adjustment under decelerating growth: The Asian experience*, Paper presented at an informal ILO expert group meeting, Geneva, 9–10 January 1986; published in ILO: *Stabilisation, adjustment and poverty*, World Employment Programme Research Working Papers on International Employment Policies, No. 1 (Geneva, 1986).

[2] ILO: *Stabilisation, adjustment and poverty*, op. cit. p. 2.

[3] A. Bhalla (ed.): *Technology and employment in industry* (Geneva, ILO; 3rd edition 1985); and idem: *Facing the technological challenge* (Geneva, ILO, 1985).

[4] S. Nigam: *Training implications of technological changes in manufacturing in new industrial countries: The case of India*, Training Policies Discussion Paper No. 16 (Geneva, ILO, 1986).

[5] Lisk, op. cit., p. 24.

[6] ibid., p. 25.

[7] Amjad, op. cit., p. 25.

[8] ILO: *Major stages and steps in energy manpower analysis: A practical framework* (Geneva, 1986), p. vi.

[9] ILO/ARTEP: *Energy manpower analysis: A manual for planners* (New Delhi, 1987).

[10] Examples are an appraisal report on industrial training in Egypt, Final Report (ILO, 1984), and an appraisal report on manpower and training requirements in the electric power sector in Ethiopia (ILO, 1984).

[11] L. Richter: "Manpower planning in developing countries: Changing approaches and emphases", in *International Labour Review* (Geneva) (Nov.–Dec. 1984).

[12] R. Blandy and S. Richardson (eds.): *How labour markets work* (Melbourne, Longman Cheshire Pty., 1982), p. 1.

[13] R. Hollister: *Manpower planning viewed as an analysis process for manpower and employment policy formation and monitoring*, Paper prepared for a Seminar on New Approaches to Manpower Analysis and Planning and Their Relevance to Indonesia, Jakarta, 1986, p. 15.

[14] G. Rodgers: *Labour markets, labour processes and economic development: Some research issues* (mimeographed World Employment Programme research working papers, Geneva, ILO, 1985; restricted).

[15] C. Dougherty: *Labour market studies and manpower development planning* (London, London School of Economics, 1983), p. 5.

¹⁶ R. Hollister: *The relevance of manpower planning in a rapidly developing economy*, ILO/ARTEP Seminar on Manpower Planning (Malaysia, Fort Dickson, 1981).

¹⁷ ILO/ARTEP: *Energy manpower analysis: a manual for planners* (New Delhi, 1987).

¹⁸ R. Hollister: *Manpower planning* . . . op. cit. p. 45.

¹⁹ J. Hilowitz: *Tracer studies as tools for identifying training needs: An evaluation*, Discussion Paper No. 4, Training Policies Programme (Geneva, ILO, 1982).

²⁰ Dougherty, op. cit. p. 14.

²¹ Kajian Perubahand Pekerjaan: *Employment Turnover Survey* (in Malay), 1st half of 1985, Perhidmatan Penerangan Pasar Buruh, Jabatan Tenaga Rakyat, Mementarian Buruh, Malaysia.

²² L. Richter: "Manpower and employment information through key informants", in *International Labour Review*, July–Aug. 1982.

²³ Department of Labour, New Zealand: *Key skills trends studies, Printing and publishing industry* (Wellington, 1984).

²⁴ R. Rao: *A technical paper on new approaches, methods and techniques in generating, managing and utilising labour market information in India*, Paper prepared for the Inter-regional Seminar on Upgrading Labour Market Information Reporting Systems in Developing Countries, Copenhagen, 13–17 October 1986, p. 30.

²⁵ ILO: *Reporting by key informants on labour markets* (Geneva, 1985).

²⁶ The term is borrowed from R. Chambers: "Rapid rural appraisal: Rationale and repertoire", in *Public administration and development*, Vol. 1, 1981, pp. 95–106, who makes the point that "while there are well-known dangers and cross-checking is necessary, key informants are a major tool for rapid rural appraisal".

²⁷ Dougherty, op. cit., p. 16.

²⁸ M. Hopkins, L. Crouch and S. Moreland: *Macbeth: A model for forecasting population, education, manpower, employment, underemployment and unemployment*, World Employment Programme research working papers, Aspects of labour market analysis and employment planning, No. 11 (Geneva, ILO, 1986).

²⁹ Hopkins, Crouch and Moreland, op. cit., p. 32.

³⁰ A. Lederer: "Information technology: 1, Planning and developing a human resources information system", in *Personnel* (New York, American Management Association), May–June 1984.

³¹ Background paper, Inter-regional Seminar on Upgrading Labour Market Information Reporting Systems in Developing Countries, Copenhagen, 13–17 October 1986, p. 21; and ILO/ARTEP: *Computerisation of labour market information*, Proceedings of an Inter-country Symposium on Labour Market Information Functions of Labour Administration, Denpasar, Indonesia, 11–19 August 1986 (Bangkok, 1987).

Chapter 5

Regional and country aspects of labour market information

A. Regional aspects

Although many of the issues discussed in the foregoing sections of this monograph are of a rather general nature, their relative importance and ways and means of dealing with them show specific regional aspects.

Awareness of the need for labour market information for various decision-making purposes is now fairly widespread. However, this seems to have originated first and found strongest expression in Asian countries. The considerable number of regional, subregional and national seminars and workshops on labour market information held in the Asian region over the past ten years bears witness to this fact. It is also substantiated by the great variety of action taken and the notable progress achieved in data availability and analysis, as can be clearly inferred from comparing the national reports prepared for subsequent seminars and workshops. Other regions saw such awareness manifesting itself at a later stage. For example, most countries in the African region are latecomers in this respect. However, they seem to have become very conscious of this late start and are greatly intensifying their interest and involvement in efforts to upgrade labour market information.[1]

Areas of emphasis with respect to the types of labour market information and the relevant data sources selected for improvement have also varied considerably. Latin America, on the whole, has attached primary importance to national-level labour market information to be obtained from household surveys. So has the Caribbean region, though to a lesser degree. This emphasis on the generation of highly aggregate labour market information is probably largely due to the primacy in these regions of the formulation of manpower and employment strategy at national level vis-à-vis relevant concern and action at subnational levels. But it also no doubt has something to do with the smallness of a number of countries, especially in the Central American and Caribbean regions. Concomitant with this orientation is a certain predilection for national labour market modelling and employment planning exercises. This goes hand in hand with a strong commitment to statistical surveys pursuing high standards of accuracy and representativeness. An important contributory reason for the strong macro-level features and the strive for statistical excellence in labour market information is undoubtedly the fact that formal labour markets in Latin America have reached larger dimensions and greater importance than in other regions of the Third World. On the other hand, but perhaps not really surprisingly so, the output of labour market information by generally weak and metropolitan-centred employment services is, as a rule, held in low esteem and is often highly suspect to policy-makers and planners.

Asia is offering a more differentiated picture in this respect. Although a number of countries in this region is also attaching importance to national labour force surveys and other statistical inquiries on manpower and employment as major inputs in the necessary data provision for national policy-making and planning, data from employment services generally play a more positively acknowledged role in this regard than in Latin America. Therefore, efforts to improve the labour market information delivery capacity of employment services appear to be somewhat stronger in the former than in the latter region. Moreover, Asian countries seem to have shown a higher propensity to widen the manpower and employment information mandate of employment services from the formal to the informal sector and from urban areas to rural areas,[2] and to improve regional and local labour market information. They also have shown a greater readiness to experiment with new approaches and methods of data collection and analysis, as previously discussed. Moreover, experiments and tests are under way in several countries in the Asian region to associate the gathering of local labour market data in the informal sector with direct promotional support and aid activities for the more vulnerable groups.

Behind these efforts lies the long-standing endeavour of many Asian countries to seek realisation of employment promotion and policy concerns with the elimination of poverty through the development of the employment potential in the informal sector, in particular in the rural areas. One important policy tool for achieving a greater impact in these directions is the devolution of planning to regional and local levels. It is surely no coincidence that some of the newer approaches to the generation of labour market information took their origin from, and have been particularly intensively tested in, the Asian region.

In contrast, labour market information has a much shorter and less intense history in most African countries. Yet employment services have gained a certain tradition in a number of African countries. Their regular reporting on announced vacancies, registered unemployment and placements has offered some quantitative labour market information in the rather small formal sector. However, in most African countries this labour market reporting has seldom contained much signalling and analytical substance. Some improvements have taken place, but at a rather slow pace. Innovative experiments have also been undertaken, though only in a few countries.[3] However, the fact that the first employment- and skill-oriented investigations into the informal sector were undertaken in several urban centres of French-speaking Africa deserves particular mention.[4]

Nation-wide collection of labour market information through household sample surveys is also held in high esteem by the majority of African countries. However, only few have the necessary resources to make more than sporadic and limited use of them. Their field of application has been primarily in the preparation of the manpower chapters of national economic development plans. In these plans the removal of critical skill bottle-necks usually occupied the most important position among different policy objectives. It is only with the fairly recent reorientation of economic policies towards fuller employment, better income distribution and the satisfaction of basic needs that new and improved data requirements in the manpower and employment fields have become more widely recognised and acted upon. However, the bulk of the efforts to upgrade labour market information capacity has been absorbed by the magnitude of the task involved in narrowing down the long list of the well-known constraints and deficiencies which continue to plague many labour market information programmes in Africa.[5]

There are also notable regional variations in the institutional framework within which labour market information activities are undertaken. This applies in particular to the nature and extent of producer-user collaboration and the respective roles of the social partners in it. However, these differences are more difficult to pinpoint. Again, institutional arrangements in the form of specially designated labour market information agencies, divisions, subdivisions, units and the like seem to be more common in Asia than in the other regions. In most cases they are subdivisions of employment services—with the already noted tendency of labour market information generation being treated as a by-product—though a certain degree of independence is noteworthy in most countries. Through tripartite advisory committees which form part of the statutory set-up of public employment services, as called for by the Employment Service Convention, 1948 (No. 88), which found ratification in quite a number of Asian countries, employers' and workers' organisations have the possibility of influencing the labour market information activities of employment services. However, really active interest in labour market information on the part of employers' and workers' organisations in Asia is none the less also of rather recent date. It certainly has received much impetus from the deepening economic crisis and its devastating effects on an already precarious employment situation as it has in other regions. While employers' interest and ability in making good use of whatever labour market information is accessible to them have become a fairly common phenomenon observable with little differences in all five regions, this cannot be said of workers' organisations. However, the Asian region, and to some extent also the Caribbean, offer a more encouraging picture in the latter respect. A greater number of trade unions in these regions has become alerted to the importance of labour market information for their decision-making. They have initiated efforts to be more closely associated with national labour market information programmes and to improve their own technical skills in analysing such information. Supporting assistance by the International Confederation of Free Trade Unions (ICFTU) has in many cases led to quite remarkable progress.

Finally, there also seem to be regional differences with respect to the involvement of research institutes and universities in the generation and analysis of labour market information. However, these variations are blurred by considerable country deviations from the average regional features. Nevertheless, it may be said that throughout the Third World the role of research institutes and universities in the generation of manpower and employment information and their analysis is rather weak. The Latin American and Asian regions offer exceptions. Research institutes in some countries of the Latin American region have played an important role in the building up of macro-economic and employment models and in related data generation and analysis as inputs in national policy-making and planning processes. In some Asian countries' research institutes, with direct mandates for manpower planning and human resources development, have been involved in making substantial inputs into the formulation of manpower and employment components or chapters of socio-economic development plans.

It may be concluded that though there are some common features, considerable variations are noticeable between different countries of the same region with regard to nature and scope of labour market information activities reflecting different degrees of severity and priorities of main manpower and employment issues, different background conditions and traditions and, last but not least, different resource endowments. This is evident from the following summary of five selected country papers which were submitted to the inter-regional seminar. This brief review will add national colour and practical dimensions to the preceding regional account.

B. Country examples

Ethiopia

Unlike the three Asian countries just discussed, Ethiopia has a rather short history in the generation and analysis of labour market information. It has started a coherent and determined programme only quite recently and from a rather weak base. These handicaps are, however, somewhat compensated by strong government commitment and notable efforts to catch up.[6]

Evidence of the awareness of the importance of manpower and employment information for human resources development and policy formulation may be primarily seen in the setting up of a tripartite Manpower and Employment Advisory Committee in 1984. It includes major users and producers of labour market information. The mandate of the Committee relating to questions of manpower and employment information generation is to—*(a)* review plans for the conduct of manpower surveys; *(b)* discuss and approve draft questionnaires; *(c)* review survey reports; *(d)* investigate unemployment and suggest measures to deal with it; *(e)* assess labour proclamations and suggest amendments, if considered necessary; *(f)* study ways and means of improving the functioning of employment services; *(g)* develop full collaboration between all ministries and organisations concerned with employment promotion; and *(h)* advise on ways and means of achieving balanced employment in both rural and urban areas.

Increasing concern with the manpower and employment issues of the country is running parallel with all-out efforts to ensure success of the Ten-Year Perspective Plan. The primary objectives of the plan are to eradicate poverty, unemployment, illiteracy and exploitation and to build up a strong self-reliant and self-sustaining economy. The need to orchestrate the national endeavour to attain these targets led the Office of the National Committee for Central Planning to set up in 1985 a parallel Inter-ministerial Committee to *(a)* take stock of the existing situation with regard to the development and use of manpower in the country and to *(b)* suggest ways and means of enhancing motivation, career development, productivity and incentives. The need for better information in all these respects was recognised by the Committee, as reflected in a number of recommendations it put forward to upgrade existing labour market information sources.

Various labour market data were collected in recent years by different ministries, agencies and organisations. A Population Census conducted in 1983/84 by the Central Statistical Office has provided benchmark data and a frame for several manpower and employment surveys and projections. The latter included manpower and housing sample surveys in Addis Ababa and 17 other larger towns in 1976 and 1978, first and second rounds of the National Sample Survey and the Rural Labour Force Survey of 1981/82, annual Industrial Surveys, the Manpower Survey of 1983/84, the School-leaver Tracer Study of 1985, the *Annual Labour Statistics Bulletin*, an annual account of "Training and manpower in Ethiopia" and various ad hoc surveys such as the survey of employment in ministries and government, and private establishments employing more than 50 persons in 1980. A special survey of skilled manpower requirements, especially managerial and highly skilled manpower in both public and private sectors, was carried on in 1983.

This is a picture of progress, though it is realised that "the scope and coverage of these studies are somewhat limited . . . and that it is hard to say that labour market information collected so far is comprehensive and complete or particularly useful".

Their main achievement is that "they have thrown some light upon the size and characteristics of the labour force available".[7]

The central development planning approach adopted by the country and the emphasis on mobilising the material and human resources of the country have been instrumental in Ethiopia's drive to establish a sound system of collecting information on the manpower and employment situation, main issues and trends. Accordingly, quite substantial resources were earmarked for programmes to be undertaken by the Ministry of Labour and the Central Statistical Office during the next fiscal years to improve information generation in the human resources field. Further manpower surveys are planned for both the formal and informal sectors to assess levels of employment, the rate of unemployment, income distribution patterns and trends in labour supply and demand. It is planned to pay particular attention to the informal sector, both in rural and urban areas. In view of the vast size of this sector, which is believed to account for more than 80 per cent of the labour force, cost considerations are looming large. Therefore, plans are under study to make fuller use of various mass organisations which were set up in the country recently such as the Urban Dwellers' Associations, the Ethiopian Peasants' Organisations and the All-Ethiopian Trade Unions. These are to collect basic information regularly on the size and composition of the workforce in the informal sector and its employment capacity "once these grass-roots organisations are fully established".[8] In addition, there is interest in adopting the key informants approach as a supplementary source of data provision. A first attempt has been made to test its applicability through a Key Informants Survey on Employment and Unemployment in a random sample of *kebeles* (urban districts) in Addis Ababa carried out in December 1986/January 1987 to obtain a better view of the nature and extent of unemployment according to sex, age, occupation and educational levels. In a provisional assessment of its results, it is stated that through this approach "applicable data may be collected very fast and cheaply".[9]

In these various efforts to upgrade labour market information activities, Ethiopia has sought and received international co-operation as, for example, in the conduct of the establishment survey, with the assistance of the International Development Association (IDA), in 1984 and for the development of manpower assessment and planning capacity through a UNDP/ILO project which terminated early in 1987. It is proposed that follow-up be provided to this project with the main objective of establishing a manpower data and labour statistics bank similar to the manpower management information system which is being developed in Indonesia.

India

India may be considered a model case of all the major issues, constraints and disappointments, as well as of the opportunities, efforts and successes associated with labour market information activities in developing countries. There is hardly a problem of labour market information which has not been encountered there. At the same time, it is difficult to think of any innovative attempt at improving labour market information delivery and analysis which has not been undertaken in India.

The sources of labour market information which were developed in India, especially after independence, are many and varied. They include—*(a)* the Population Census conducted by the Registrar General of India; *(b)* the Employment Market Information Programme of the Ministry of Labour (Employment Exchanges); *(c)* the quinquennial Surveys of Labour Force, Employment and Unemployment by the

National Sample Survey Organisation; *(d)* the annual Surveys of Industries and Factory Surveys conducted by the Labour Bureau; *(e)* data collection on the socio-economic characteristics of beneficiaries of various rural development programmes such as the Integrated Rural Development Programme, the National Rural Employment Programme, the Rural Landless Employment Guarantee Programme, etc.; *(f)* the Economic Census conducted by the Central Statistical Organisation; *(g)* enrolment data from educational and training institutions; *(h)* data generation of the Small-Industry Organisation, Khadi and Village Industries, etc.; and *(i)* manpower and employment surveys and studies, including Area Skills Surveys, carried out by government and non-governmental agencies and institutions.[10]

Since data generation of these various agencies is decentralised and largely uncoordinated, concepts, definitions and frequency of the surveys, investigations and studies differ considerably so that comparison between data from different sources is difficult, if not impossible. A solution has not yet been found to another major problem of long standing, to which attention is often drawn: the important delays that are occurring in the processing and publication of manpower and employment information documents, especially the quarterly and annual employment surveys. This severely limits signalling potential and usefulness for operational decision-making.

Lack of full coverage has also remained a major preoccupation in labour market information activities. Many experiments have been made to cope with this problem. Some of them have faltered mainly because of the lack of adequate resources. The attempted coverage of private sector establishments employing between five and nine workers is an example. Others were given up because they are considered to have failed to produce the hoped-for results or to meet acceptable standards of accuracy and reliability. A number of experiments continue to be pursued, such as the use of data from the integrated rural development programme at district and block levels and the scheme for promoting self-employment in the urban areas to generate labour market information in the informal sector in both rural and urban areas. New initiatives such as the conduct of "mixed surveys" and the setting up of mobile teams to collect labour market information in areas not covered by the labour market information programme of the Ministry of Labour are under way. It has also been suggested that employment and unemployment information at district and development block levels could be improved through better analysis of the data generated by the quinquennial Surveys of Labour Force. However, doubts have been expressed whether this could produce signals sufficiently useful without an enormous increase in sample size.[11]

Among these many-sided efforts, there are two of priority ranking. These are likely to have a considerable impact on further progress in labour market information capacity. The first is computerisation of the operations of employment services on the basis of a gradually expanding programme in which resources input is shared between the central Government and state governments which are willing to participate in this programme. The second is a general programme of overhauling the labour market intelligence component of the employment services.

As part of the latter programme, it is intended to develop further, within selected employment services offices, the so-called "self-employment pilot project cells". At the same time, the rural employment information and assistance bureaux, which are entrusted with the provision of comprehensive labour market information at regular intervals, are to serve both the rural informal sector and the urban informal sector. These innovations aim at making labour market information an effective tool of an integrated manpower services delivery system. The intention is to help persons in need of employment assistance through guidance about locally available employment and self-employment opportunities, through facilitating access to credit and other services and through personalised placement activities in employment or self-employment in collaboration with the local authorities in charge of development and employment promotion programmes.[12]

Both employers' and workers' organisations in India have shown an active interest in making their own contribution to the national effort to upgrade labour market information capability. On the employers' side, the Research Bureau of the Employers' Federation of India has started to compile labour market information of importance to employers in a data bank made possible by the donation of computer facilities by the Norwegian Employers' Federation. The Bureau has plans in hand to prepare research monographs on major labour market issues viewed from the employers' standpoint. The workers' organisations as well have activated their plans to step up the gathering and analysis of labour market information. The Indian Trade Union Congress, with substantial support from the ICFTU, has provided training on labour market information to its research staff and undertook in 1984 a major labour market study in the steel-producing and steel-processing centre of Jamshedpur in the state of Bihar. An outside observer expressed the following opinion on this study: "There have been limitations, . . . but despite these the report is not only balanced but at all stages it proceeds on the basis and assumption that productivity, creation of more employment and jobs and the quality of working life are all interwoven and that to achieve these it is necessary that employers and workmen think and act together and enjoy the fruits thereof in common".[13]

A somewhat unique position in labour market information generation and analysis is held by the Institute of Applied Manpower Research (IAMR). This is a semi-public research body with all interested ministries, professional organisations and educational institutions represented on its General Council. As its name indicates, it is foremost concerned with studies and research which are to yield results for practical use. With its main mandate to advance knowledge about the nature, characteristics and use of human resources in India, it has often taken a leading and unifying role in orienting labour market research and reporting towards problems and issues of current major concern. The testing of the key informants approach in selected areas of two states, the development of a national manpower and skills inventory, the establishment of a data bank for technical manpower and various sectoral and subsectoral manpower surveys, studies of manpower development in rural areas— these are only a few relevant examples of a vast programme. Moreover, activities of the Institute also include the holding of training courses, often with an international dimension, for various actors in the labour market. Finally, the work of the Institute as a back-up to policy-making has found recognition in its being entrusted with the preparation of background papers on manpower, employment and labour market issues as an important input into the formulation of the Indian Five-Year Plans.

Both in terms of the great variety of problems encountered and the many ways and means attempted to deal with them, the Indian labour market information mechanism and its functioning provides a rich observation and training ground for other developing countries. This potential is enhanced by an experienced training structure provided by such institutions as IAMR and the Training Centre for Employment Services Staff (CIRTES), which have organised a large number of training courses on labour market information and related subjects for Indian as well as for foreign students and fellows.

Indonesia

The generation and analysis of labour market information in Indonesia have much in common with those of the two Asian countries reviewed above although in this case they had a later start and have thus reached a lesser degree of diversion. The main sources of data and their problems are very similar. Inadequacies of existing information such as partial coverage (excluding the large informal sector), lack of timeliness, high levels of aggregation, duplication of efforts and, above all, the absence of an effective co-ordination mechanism are also major problems which have become accentuated by resource constraints. On top of these, new data claims caused by the economic recession and the concomitant structural adjustment efforts have created additional demands. There has thus been a search for new sources of data which are essential for these purposes, which are cost-effective and which supplement meaningfully existing data of the traditional type.

On the other hand, labour market information activities in Indonesia have some special features. The first is the position which has been assigned to labour market information as an integral part of an overall comprehensive Manpower Management Information System. This was established a few years ago with international co-operation. Its primary objective is to facilitate decision- and policy-making processes within the Ministry of Manpower in all areas of its responsibility. However, it is also intended to be of service to other manpower and employment information users. The second particular characteristic is that computerisation of all relevant data flows is attempted to form an integral part of the above-mentioned system. Initial emphasis is being placed on the following data sets—*(a)* manpower emigration (international labour placement scheme); *(b)* labour market information provided regularly through the reporting of the Ministry's 200-odd regional and local Manpower Offices; *(c)* government employment records; *(d)* foreign manpower registrations; *(e)* labour absorption; *(f)* migration between the different regions of Indonesia; *(g)* labour-intensive projects; *(h)* total employment in each sector of the economy; *(i)* enrolment and output of vocational training institutions and centres; *(j)* work disputes; *(k)* new-style labour programmes and collective bargaining; *(l)* work accidents; *(m)* social security; *(n)* inspections of factories and plantations; *(o)* multi-purpose data; *(p)* establishment surveys; *(q)* Department of Manpower personnel; and *(r)* inventory.

It has already been mentioned that this list of items is of primary concern to the tasks and responsibilities and to the management functions of the Ministry of Manpower and, to a large extent, also to the interests of the employers' and workers' organisations. However, it is planned to extend this "priority list" to include "relevant data files from outside sources" for other users.[14]

The third special feature of labour market information activities in Indonesia is their support by a longer-term United Nations Development Programme (UNDP)/ILO technical co-operation project which started in the late seventies. The project is lending support to both the data generation and computerisation parts of the emerging manpower management information system.

The origin and development of this joint undertaking offers many important lessons, insights and hindsights concerning the main issues and problems involved in the setting up of a computer-supported labour market information system and of the prerequisites which need to be fulfilled. If one single lesson stands out, it is the recognition that planning and target setting for a national labour market information system should not be based on considerations of what is desirable and should be done, but rather on what could be done on the basis of clearly identified priorities and available resources. In other words, a step-by-step programme of improvement would seem preferable to an ambitious plan of inputs, outputs and activities. This is all the more important if, as is the case in Indonesia, a labour market information programme takes off from a rather weak base.

It is something of a paradox that Indonesia possesses a strong potential foundation for producing operationally useful labour market information. This basis was laid in the early fifties with the opening of 27 regional manpower offices. In the meantime, the network was strengthened by the addition of some 170 subregional and local offices. Under the above-mentioned project, and mainly prompted by a worsening employment situation giving rise to more concern with regional employment planning and its interaction with national employment policy, action is being taken in several ways to strengthen the network of regional manpower offices for three interrelated purposes: first, as generators of labour market signals, secondly, as centres for regional and local labour market analysis and, thirdly, as focal points for regional employment planning. Essential ingredients of such action are the reorientation of the existing reporting system of the manpower offices from a mainly administrative type of reporting to more purposeful labour market signalling and analysis and a greatly stepped-up training effort for the staff involved in these activities.

With regard to the first, modified forms for local and regional labour market reporting and analysis have been prepared which await practical application—on an experimental and limited scale in the first instance. Moreover, a unifying labour market information model was worked out. This proposes to make this modified reporting system the centre-piece of a national labour market information network into which other relevant information flows can be channelled. The main aim is to set in motion a "two-way flow of data and information . . . essential for achieving both regional and national plan objectives".[15]

With respect to the second part, staff training in labour market reporting and analysis is to be greatly intensified. This objective ranks high in the priority list of activities foreseen in the next two-year programme of the Manpower Management Information System project. A basic training programme for a core group of ten trainers has been prepared and is due to start shortly. These trainers are to run training courses for medium-level technical personnel of regional and subregional manpower offices on the basis of training material that is being developed during the trainers' training course in the light of experience gained from training material prepared for the course.

While the focus of measures for improvement has so far been mainly on upgrading and extending sources of manpower and employment information already in existence, there was a growing recognition that the time and resources required to attain full coverage and adequate standards of such sources were beyond levels that could be readily afforded. Therefore, the Ministry of Manpower decided to test a number of new approaches: key informants surveys, analysis of job advertisements in newspapers and tracer studies. These experiments have not yet reached a conclusive stage to permit well-founded decisions about applying as a whole—or in part—for integration into the national labour market information network.

Some steps have also been taken towards bringing about a closer collaboration between main users and producers of labour market information. A first step was the conduct of a survey (functional analysis) among different units of the Ministry of Manpower to take stock of existing data generation and flows of information, the use made of the information and of future needs. The subsequent step was to extend this stock-taking exercise to the regional level of the activities of the Ministry of Manpower, i.e. to the regional manpower offices, and in particular to the employers' and workers' organisations. This was one of the major objectives of a National Seminar on Labour Market Information held in 1985. The seminar proved to be particularly fruitful in providing a convenient tripartite forum of discussions and exchange of views. It led to the clear formulation of the need for essential labour market information and an articulation of the purposes for which it was to be used. It was concluded that this inititative required regular follow-up and gradual extension so as to include in future seminars other important labour market information users. There was some hope expressed that this seminar would constitute a first stage in a continuous process of improved user-producer collaboration, which by all concerned was recognised as being of vital importance for the relevance and usefulness of labour market information.

Involvement of universities and research institutions in labour market information activities has not been notable for important contributions, with perhaps the exception of the University of Jogjakarta and the University of Indonesia, Jakarta. There is no doubt ample room for a closer collaboration of research institutes in the generation of labour market information and in-depth analysis. This is why the Manpower Management Information System project has recently sought to establish closer links with the above-mentioned universities.

Malaysia

One of the most characteristic features of the very active labour market information programme of Malaysia might be seen in the cautious step-by-step approach which was followed in its expansion and consolidation. Moreover, the propensity of the programme to experiment and to innovate is also noteworthy. It may be said further that the programme has attained a level of relevance and quality which is not easily matched by other labour market information programmes in the region and in other developing countries in general.[16]

One of the most impressive recent outputs of the programme is the initiation of biannual National Labour and Manpower Reports in 1983/84. The two issues so far published highlight the situation, main issues and trends of the labour market in Malaysia and its major regions covering population and the labour force, employment and unemployment, manpower development, labour market functioning and signalling, labour productivity, wages and other related subjects and those for which the Ministry of Labour is responsible. Special chapters analyse subjects of current major concern at greater depth.[17]

The main sources of labour market information include—*(a)* the Population Census; *(b)* the quarterly conducted, but only annually published, Labour Force Surveys; *(c)* the annual Surveys of Selected Industries; *(d)* the annual Census of Selected Industries—all these are conducted by the Statistics Department; *(e)* the monthly Manpower Bulletins; *(f)* the quarterly conducted, but only semi-annually published, Employment Turnover Surveys; *(g)* Sectoral Surveys; *(h)* the annual Survey of Employment and Earnings; *(i)* triannual Occupational Wage Surveys—all of the latter carried out under the responsibility of the Ministry of Labour. Other sources of labour market information are the Annual Report of the Malaysian Industrial Development Authority, the Annual Report of the Ministry of Finance and the Five-Year Malaysian Plan Book, published by the Economic Planning Unit.

Much of the information obtained from these surveys and reports is highly aggregated. This has been recognised and efforts are being made to adapt labour market information activities more effectively to regional and district development planning, which in recent years has received increasing emphasis with policies of decentralisation and of developing the informal sector, both in rural and urban areas. However, the continued recession has had adverse effects on the availability of resources. Allocations for meeting these new needs have therefore not been forthcoming on an adequate scale. Attention has thus been concentrated on making fuller use of existing sources of information. This has included efforts to bring about better coverage, to avoid overlap and duplication, to disaggregate industrial and occupational classifications, to make a geographical breakdown of nationally presented labour market data and to improve the timeliness and accessibility of available labour market information through the preparation and regular upgrading of a Directory of Labour Market Information.

At the same time, some experiments have continued to develop simple and practical labour market signalling devices at acceptable cost levels. One of these devices, selected labour turnover surveys, has already been referred to earlier. Another device, the key informants approach, was tested a few years ago in a detailed survey in two villages. The approach, as a whole, has not been found suitable for general application, but elements of it have been made use of in another innovative activity of the labour market information programme. New sectoral and subsectoral surveys were recently initiated by the Ministry of Labour to assess the employment outlook, the occupational profiles and the training requirements of selected industrial subsectors. The latter included an assessment of the extent to which on-the-job or in-service training practised was taken into account to determine the needs for formal training programmes. The new survey series also seeks to trace occupational changes brought about by the introduction of new technology and production processes. These changes are to be made known expeditiously to industrial/vocational training institutes, as guidance for their programmes and courses to provide for different manpower needs.

It seems that this new survey experienced certain teething troubles. Rather low response rates from the industry was one of these. In an effort to compensate for it, the key informants approach was introduced in this survey by conducting personal interviews with production managers, personnel managers and training officers from selected firms. This yielded more specific information about prevailing employment practices such as hiring methods, sources of recruitment and the nature and extent of training provided by the firms themselves.

A major problem which continues to have a retarding effect on the "development of a comprehensive labour market information system" is the absence of a firmly established collaboration and co-ordination device. The formation of a "linkage between labour market information producers and users . . . in the form of a formally recognised committee would be the logical option towards a programmed improvement in the system".[18]

Recent administrative changes have led to the taking of a greater initiative on the part of the Economic Planning Unit of the Prime Minister's Office in matters of manpower planning and labour market information. This new development might pave the way for establishing such co-ordination.

Both employers' and workers' organisations have shown keen interest in the setting-up of an effectively working co-ordinating and collaborating mechanism. Employers' interest has undoubtedly been activated by the recent preparation of an Industrial Master Plan, one of the main public policy responses to the continuing economic contraction and the dwindling role of the public sector as a major provider of employment opportunities. In this plan, manpower planning and training needs assessment have come to be viewed as a closely and continuously inter-related activity of training, target setting and the monitoring of these targets. If these tasks are to be made the primary responsibility of the private sector itself, as has been proposed, employers' interest in the generation of purposeful labour market information and their own contribution to this end is likely to intensify.

The workers' side is particularly concerned to participate fully in the national labour market information programme. Its primary interest at present is to be objectively informed and to be up to date regarding the repercussions of the recent economic downturn on employment of the wage-earning labour force. It realises that without proper information on impending layoffs and planned counter-action on the part of the Government and industry, the stand and position taken by the workers vis-à-vis remedial policies and measures lack factual evidence to be bolstered up. In addition, it is also cognisant of the fact that in order to do a more satisfactory job in this respect, it needs to equip itself with better skills regarding labour market generation and analysis. Therefore, it has initiated with the help of the ICFTU a programme to improve its ability in canvassing labour market issues, in preparing reports and surveys and in ensuring their wide distribution.

It is not quite clear to what extent universities and research institutes in Malaysia are involved in a substantial and systematic way in contributing to the generation and analysis labour market information. There are examples of important ad hoc involvement such as the recent study of the transition process between the formal world of education and the world of work, undertaken jointly by the University of Malaysia and the International Institute of Educational Planning.[19] However, it seems that there is room for improvement in order to strengthen the research input to a national labour market information programme.

Zimbabwe

At the time of independence in 1980, Zimbabwe had a dualistic system of labour market information. There were separate employment services, training facilities, wages, working conditions and trade unions for Africans and Europeans with separate information mechanisms. Moreover, the emphasis of information generation activities was on wage earning in the formal sector, where White settlers were in the majority, to the virtual exclusion of the large informal sector, which was entirely African.[20]

The National Manpower Survey (NMS) undertaken soon after independence heralded a profound change in this system. The main objectives of this survey were to assess the size, characteristics and areas of skill shortages of the total manpower resources of the country and to formulate, on the basis of the results of this survey, both short- and long-term training policies. Moreover, the survey was to clarify the skill categorisation used in previous labour market studies, as well as the wider issue of the professional, managerial and other high-level occupations, where there was a preponderance of Whites, in relation to the new policies pursued by the independent country. Based on the insights gained from this survey, a number of immediate measures were taken. One of them was the setting up of an Inter-ministerial Recruitment Committee to introduce the control of foreign recruitment. This permitted only the immigration of persons of those occupational categories for which the National Manpower Survey had signalled critical shortage conditions. An Annual Review of Manpower (ARM) undertaken jointly by the Ministries of Labour, Manpower Planning and Social Welfare was introduced to update this information.

Since the holding of the basic manpower survey, a considerable number of other labour market information sources have been developed. Sources of labour market information in Zimbabwe now include—*(a)* the Population Census; *(b)* the Manpower Survey; *(c)* quarterly employment inquiries and an annual Employment Census; *(d)* the Informal Sector Survey; *(e)* the Industrial Census, *(f)* national accounts; *(g)* a national trade union survey; *(h)* an evaluation report of primary school drop-outs in Zimbabwe (1978–84); *(i)* a tracer study of GCE "A" and "O" level students; *(j)* unemployment statistics obtained from the public employment service and private employment agencies; and *(k)* statistics on number of students abroad, number of foreigners employed and work permits issued, industrial disputes and social security. This information is processed by the Central Statistical Office which published it in the *Monthly Statistical Bulletin.*

In spite of substantial progress, those responsible for labour market information feel that "there are still serious lacunae in the collection of data on human resources development". There is a need for more detailed information on *(a)* critical skill shortages to facilitate both effective control of foreign recruitment and a more accurate assessment of scholarship requirements; *(b)* the training programmes conducted in the private sector in order to know the rate of progress made to rectify racial imbalances; *(c)* income distribution since the statistics available from the Central Statistical Office are too highly aggregated; and *(d)* employment levels and, in particular, unemployment since the only providers of such information are the private and public employment services. Under present circumstances, these present only a partial picture of the situation.

The most recent additions to the stock of labour market information fill some of the gaps. A labour force survey, the first of its kind, was launched early in 1986 in the context of the Zimbabwe National Household Survey Capability Programme. It collected information on, inter alia, sex, civil status, citizenship, ethnic group, previous residence, educational level completed, training, current activity status and employment status. A significant feature of the survey was the consultative role which an inter-ministerial and tripartite committee played in the planning and the conduct of the survey. Similarly, a national survey of job evaluation and classification, which was launched in 1986, was also mounted with the assistance of a tripartite committee.

This close association of the social partners with manpower and employment surveys takes Zimbabwe somewhat ahead of other African countries and of developing countries in general. Though such collaboration does not yet extend to the whole fabric of the labour market information mechanism, the way is traced for continuous progress. Paradoxically, while both employers' and workers' organisations are associated with the labour market information generation process, they do not seem to have fully seized the opportunity offered by such collaboration.[21]

As far as the involvement of university institutes in the collection and analysis of labour market information is concerned, there was an active participation of the Department of Economics in the conduct of the informal sector survey. Moreover, it is reported that dissertations on labour market and employment issues are also being carried out in this institute by post-graduate students.

On the whole, there has been little interest and activity in Zimbabwe regarding new approaches to labour market information. At the same time, the increasing concern shown by so many other developing countries with the development of the employment potential of the informal sector has found only a faint echo in Zimbabwe. One of these, the key informants approach, seems to have met with considerable scepticism on the part of two main producers and users of labour market information, the Planning and Research Section of the Ministry of Labour and the Central Statistical Office. Part of this sceptical attitude might perhaps be due to unfamiliarity with the pros and cons of the key informants approach. However, it also appears to have something to do with a certain reservation towards innovation. This is reflected in the stated view that . . . "such approaches sometimes are old misconceptions ensconced in new techniques in which case there develops a fetish of techniques and a predilection for every new fad that removes us from the central problem . . .".[22]

The main thrust of the present labour market information programme in Zimbabwe is towards making labour market phenomena and inter-relationships more transparent and achieving this through "dynamic analysis". In this context, it is proposed to place issues such as the development of the informal sector and concepts such as vulnerable groups in the labour market into the broader perspective of employment processes and their rural and urban, formal and informal connotations and inter-relationships. In brief, the central mandate of the labour market information progamme is to gear the data generation and analysis process to an understanding of such inter-relationships in support of immediate and medium-term policy decisions in the field of human resources development and use and to avoid a mere quantitative accumulation of manpower and employment statistics.

It might be added that in spite of certain differences in labour market issues experienced by Zimbabwe, this orientation of labour market information activities fits well into the new universally observed trend towards attaching more importance to labour market signalling and analysis than to the conventional manpower planning exercises.

Notes

[1] ILO/Jaspa: *The challenge of employment and basic needs in Africa*, Essays in honour of S. Nigam and to mark the tenth anniversary of JASPA. Nairobi, Oxford University Press (1986).

[2] ILO/ARTEP: *An aid to self-employment promotion by employment services in Asia and the Pacific* (Bangkok, 1968).

[3] Key informants test projects were undertaken in Somalia and Madagascar.

[4] One of the earliest surveys of this kind is discussed in G. Nihan and R. Jourdain: "The modern informal sector in Nouakchott", in *International Labour Review*, Nov.–Dec. 1978.

[5] The main technical and administrative constraints which limit the usefulness of labour market information in African countries are summarised in E. C. Iwuji: *Manpower planning and labour market*

information in Africa, Technical study No. 7, Paper prepared for the Inter-regional Seminar on Upgrading Labour Market Information Reporting Systems in Developing Countries, Copenhagen, 13–17 October 1986.

[6] U. Bedada: *A study of new approaches, methods and techniques in generating, managing and utilising labour market information in Ethiopia*, Paper prepared for the Inter-regional Seminar on Upgrading Labour Market Information Reporting Systems in Developing Countries, Copenhagen, 13–17 October 1986.

[7] ibid., pp. 3 and 8.

[8] ibid., p. 7.

[9] UNDP/ILO: *Draft report on key informants surveys on employment/unemployment* (Addis Ababa, Ministry of Labour and Social Affairs, 1987), p. 12.

[10] Rao, op cit., p. 32.

[11] ibid., p. 31.

[12] It might be mentioned that developing the "service function" of employment services or exchanges, combining information gathering, analysis and its purposeful use for employment promotion activities, has also been the subject of intensive experimentation in Bangladesh. It is also one of the important items of the present work progamme of ARPLA.

[13] *Economic Times* (Calcutta), 6 Oct. 1985.

[14] Y. Swasono and G. van Toledo: *New approaches, methods and techniques in generating, managing and utilising labour market information—The Indonesian case*, Paper prepared for the Inter-regional Seminar on Upgrading Labour Market Information Reporting Systems in Developing Countries, Copenhagen, 13–17 October 1986.

[15] ibid., p. 15.

[16] M. Alias: *New approaches, methods and techniques in generating, managing and utilising labour market information—The Malaysian Case*, Paper prepared for the Inter-regional Seminar on Upgrading Labour Market Information Reporting Systems in Developing Countries, Copenhagen, 13–17 October 1986.

[17] Ministry of Labour, Malaysia: *Labour and Manpower Report 1983/84*, op cit.

[18] Alias, *New approaches . . .* , op cit. p. 10.

[19] ibid., p. 10.

[20] B. Raftopoulos: *New approaches, methods and techniques in generating, managing and utilising labour market information in Zimbabwe*, Paper prepared for the Inter-regional Seminar on Upgrading Labour Market Information Reporting Systems in Developing Countries, Copenhagen, 13–17 October 1986.

[21] Nigam, op. cit., pp. 41 and 44.

[22] Raftopoulos, op. cit., p. 3.

Chapter 6

Conclusions: Implications for policy-oriented action

The primary task of the last chapter of this monograph is to put together the main conclusions, insights and messages which emerged from the inter-regional seminar and its five preceding regional components. This assessment will be placed against the background of the broad progress made by the longer-term ILO programme of upgrading labour market reporting capacity in the developing countries. These insights and messages may help to provide guidance for narrowing down problems and issues to those of highest priority, for identifying the most promising ways and means of dealing with them and for pointing to those technical co-operation activities which could lend effective support to such problem-solving.

A. Main insights and messages

It has become a widely accepted proposition that labour market information should not be thought of in the traditional and rather limited sense of the reporting of employment services on the functioning of formal labour markets. Rather, its coverage should extend to the total labour force of a country and its composition/distribution by economic activities, occupations and regions or localities, as well as by formal and informal sector. It should provide adequate knowledge of manpower and employment situations, issues and trends and clarify the underlying reasons and inter-relationships of labour market distortions or imbalances—as a basis for decision-making of a great variety of actors in the labour market. The usefulness for decision-making in the broad fields of manpower and employment policy must therefore be the major criterion for judging the value of any labour market information programme. Considering the rather weak basis from which many developing countries have to start to develop a comprehensive labour market information programme of the above coverage, progress could not be expected to be made on all fronts at a satisfactory rate. Therefore, priorities had to be set dealing first with information gaps which were most severely felt. In practically all developing countries, such gaps were most acute in the informal sector, both in rural and urban areas, because of its large size and the employment potential inherent in it.

It also has become quite clear that no labour market information programme can reasonably be expected to reach a stage where it may be said that the job is done in the sense that all users' needs are fully met at all times. As labour markets are in constant movement—not to say disarray—and new manpower and employment issues arise in permanent succession, labour market information has to keep abreast with such changes and adjust the content and emphasis of the programme accordingly. In other words, labour market information programmes have to be flexible to respond expeditiously to changing demands and relative priority needs.

A consensus is also emerging that a plurality of methods, techniques and approaches in the generation and analysis of labour market information is preferable to too much faith being placed in a single method, technique or approach. In this context, it was generally felt that labour market signalling and regular analysis work needed further strengthening vis-à-vis the mechanistic, projection-based manpower planning activities which had dominated in the past. Briefly, the main tasks of such analysis work would be to make the functioning of labour markets and arising or persisting imbalances and their underlying factors more transparent, to identify main manpower and employment issues and processes, to work out possibilities and options of remedial policies and measures on the basis of such knowledge and to monitor their implementation.

There have been persistent pleas from many sides that labour market information programmes should be planned and integrated into the wider framework of the overall development planning mechanism. Labour markets had to be considered integral parts of the wider socio-economic system in which production and services, labour development and utilisation and income generation interacted. Fulfilment of this prerequisite will help to keep available labour market information data continuously under review from the point of view of their adequacy for analysis and their relevance to decision- and policy-making. It is only if the process of information generation and analysis becomes systematic and purposeful that "the quality of data will show any meaningful improvement".[1]

The above insights and observations point to a number of integrative or converging prerequisites which have become more clearly identified over the past ten years of promotional activities undertaken by the longer-term ILO programme for the upgrading of labour market information capacity in developing countries. These prerequisites were reconfirmed by the inter-regional seminar, which also called attention to their central importance for a comprehensive and purposeful labour market information programme.

B. The need for convergence

The first convergence that is needed relates to the macro- and micro-levels of labour market information. The recent shifts of manpower and employment policy concerns and emphasis have entailed a greater propensity of labour market information activities to carry data generation to more disaggregated levels, i.e. to different economic sectors, occupations or occupational groups and regions/areas/localities. The question is not to argue which one is more important than the other, but to appreciate the different significance of each for different labour market actors. Macro-level labour market information underpins national manpower and employment policy-making, while micro-level labour market information is needed for operational and managerial decision-making, especially at project and local levels where national policy objectives are concretised. A two-way flow of information, i.e. a feedback mechanism, is required, downwards to give policy directives from the centre to the lower levels, and upwards to relate the impact of policy, problems and requirements back to the centre for necessary policy realignments.

A second, related convergence which should be attained is that of labour market information assessing the issues likely to emerge in the future (forecasting, projections) and signalling current situations, constraints and trends (continuous reporting). Many manpower and employment policy decisions involve longer-term gestation periods such as the construction of buildings for training centres or the training of engineers. Decision-making in these and similar cases have to be based on some sort of a preview of what the future holds. In fact, such decisions are often relying on what may be called implicit forecasting. On the other hand, many decisions demand quickness in information delivery. It appears that effectiveness of both projection and signalling work could be greatly enhanced if they were brought together in a "rolling adjustment model".

Analogously, a third convergence is called for regarding labour market research and labour market reporting. The latter keeps track of visible or easily recognisable events and changes in the labour market, especially those relating to suddenly arising or threatening imbalances in manpower supply and demand and, more generally, employment and unemployment levels. Such signals often suffice to indicate the nature and scope of the problem at hand and of the kind of short-term policy measures required to deal with it. However, more complex phenomena and the underlying causes and inter-relationships influencing labour market outcomes less visibly—but not necessarily less profoundly—are the domain of labour market research; for example, subjects for such research include government legislation and regulations, wage-fixing machinery, employer-worker relations and their bargaining positions, socially conditioned customs and practices and their impact on labour market functioning and individual or group decision-making. In addition, research has the task of probing more deeply into the longer-term facets of employment processes such as the transitions which occur during individual life cycles: from school and training to working life, from one job to another and from one locality to another, and the incentives and obstacles which either hinder or promote these moves.[2] Both signalling and research work are vital for effective manpower and employment policy-making and planning and for their translation into operational decision-making. Labour market information is likely to lack perspective, explanatory and reasoning power, on the one hand, and to be burdened with too many studies and surveys removed from reality and devoid of policy- and decision-making usefulness, on the other hand, if labour market signalling and labour market research largely ignore each other.

A fourth convergence worth striving for is that of blending quantitative with qualitative labour market information. It is widely accepted that in order to be meaningful many labour market data demand interpretation and supplementing by qualitative information such as perceptions, attitudes and motivations impinging on labour market behaviour. Orders or ranges of magnitude and directions of change might throw a bridge between the two.

Moreover, the state of deficiency in which labour market data generation finds itself in many developing countries—and the impossibility from the resources point of view to remedy this situation at an early date—makes it necessary to look for cost-effective, qualitative information sources to supplement the weak statistical basis.

It is this set of messages, insights and prerequisites which points to those critical areas of upgrading labour market reporting which may call for priority action in the next few years. These critical areas were the following—*(a)* bringing about full and continuous collaboration between producers and users; *(b)* improving the skills of those engaged in the generation and analysis of manpower and employment information; *(c)* exploiting more fully existing labour market information sources; *(d)* making better provision for meeting the needs of the informal sector for manpower and employment data; and *(e)* introducing electronic data processing facilities into labour market information handling.

C. Key areas of future action

Making collaboration between users and producers work effectively must be considered basic to the solution of both old and new problems in labour market information. Without close co-ordination of the activities of the two, there is little hope for the full integration of labour market information generation and analysis into the overall socio-economic development planning process, for a proper feedback from users to producers to ensure purposefulness of the data generated, and for earmarking adequate resources for labour market information activities.

All this has been pointed out many times before. Moreover, it cannot be said that awareness of the need for such collaboration is lacking. It is something of a paradox that there is no shortage of advisory, inter-ministerial and tripartite committees, task forces, councils, and so on, which have been established, obviously with good intentions. However in most cases they have not lived up to expectations. Many of these co-ordinating structures have turned out to be either too weak or too sporadic in their action to have any lasting effects. Specific suggestions and exhortations for changing this unsatisfactory state of affairs have not been lacking—but to little avail.

Obviously, there does not exist any patent solution of the problem, though a few useful pointers have clearly emerged from the experience of ILO programmes and seminars. It seems that committee or co-ordinating work has a better chance of functioning as a collaborative device if it is not too unwieldly and concrete programmes are established jointly setting specific tasks for the different members for given periods. The active performance of most steering committees organised for the preparation of national labour market reports for the regional seminars underlines this point. They had a specific task to perform and they were small. Therefore, the establishment of a co-ordinating mechanism—possibly starting with a small number and expanding gradually—should be based on a jointly worked out routine annual programme. This must specify the tasks to be performed by each member and provide for well-phased and interlinked activities. Whatever ministry or government agency is entrusted with primary responsibility for this co-ordination mechanism, it had better assume this in the letter and spirit of a *primus inter pares* and promoter rather than in an authoritarian manner.[3] Attempts at co-ordination based merely on regulation have in any case not been particularly successful.

National labour market information seminars or workshops, with a limited composition of government, employers' and workers' representatives in the first instance, might provide a useful initial step for building up an effective co-ordination structure. An important concomitant requirement is that it is served by a strong secretariat and that regular follow-up is a built-in feature. Willingness and readiness for full and continued collaboration will also be greatly enhanced if each member contributes to and receives from this joint exercise a credible and usable product. This can only be ensured by the participation in this collaboration of staff and personnel who are competent and well trained in the labour market information field.

The essential need for improving the skill level of staff engaged in labour market information activities has received increasing attention in recent years in many developing countries, although the actual effort made has fallen far short of needs, with a few exceptions.[4] Two of the main conditions of a successful training effort were rarely met: the availability of well-trained trainers and of appropriate training material. As a result, the body of knowledge about what makes a successful training programme in terms of content, composition, duration and didactic support is still rather thin. Well-tested prototypes of such programmes are yet to emerge. On the training material side, internationally prepared training manuals and guides of the framework type are available. However, they will need translation, adaptation and completion with practical examples from each particular country situation to be of full use.

Skill deficits are most severely felt at medium-level technical personnel ranges, i.e. the staff category which has the basic responsibilities in the "daily chores" of labour market information generation and analysis. This does not apply to government staff alone, but also to private sector personnel handling manpower and employment matters, including staff of the research and planning units of employers' and workers' organisations.

More rapid progress in the improvement of staff skills is particularly urgent for making better use of existing labour market information sources and for exploring and exploiting new sources. This must be accompanied by better user-producer collaboration, as only this will permit a full inventory of available published and unpublished information and its best possible use, especially by comparisons and cross-references.

On the other hand, this process should also include the weeding out of data which serve little or no useful purpose and which are not worth collecting. It has been said that it is much easier to demand more information than it is to abstain from doing so.[5] And, in fact, it is difficult to find an example where an effort has been made to identify and eliminate the unnecessary and the useless. It might be "cost-effective" not to overlook this activity in the future efforts of upgrading labour market information capability.

It is also in this spirit of cost-effectiveness that the demand for new data need to be examined. A cautionary remark, already made a number of years ago, needs repeating here: there is a tendency that "each time a curiosity or a new interpretation of reality develops, or a new fad emerges", new additional burdens are heaped on the labour market information system.[6] This needs to be carefully assessed. Considerations of cost-effectiveness alone are important enough. Furthermore, changes in data collection often result in detrimental consequences on comparability at both national and international levels.

On the other hand, there are easily justifiable claims for new data, especially with regard to the documentation and monitoring of new policy orientations and the emergence of new manpower and employment issues and with respect to the still largely unfulfilled labour market information needs of the informal sector. However, the difficulties encountered in providing useful manpower and employment information in this sector are not only due to the inadequacy of conventional labour market information sources and resources constraints but also to a lack of clear operational definition of what this sector stands for.

In view of these difficulties, it has been proposed that there should be less concern with the concept of the informal sector since "the attempt to describe the sector in some general physical sense is essentially mistaken and fruitless".[7] The argument continues that there would appear to be much greater reward in looking at industrial branches and sectors as a whole.[8] In this connection, studies are suggested to obtain information on the growth opportunities and constraints of the small producers in the sector/branch in question, the linkages between them and the larger firms, the incidence and nature of subcontracting by the informal sector units, the transfer of technology to small firms and the composition and development of demand for their products and services. These would cast more light on the dynamics of formal sector activities than the kind of surveys so far undertaken. The list of suggested items of information will tend to be long in practically all developing countries. Therefore, particular importance needs to be attached to ascertaining main needs and to set priorities, within the framework of the overall national labour market information programme, before any efforts to procure new data get under way. Here again, the need for the closest possible user-producer collaboration is too obvious to be once more evoked. Perhaps special target group studies and the wider use of key informants techniques might be a realistic beginning of new data initiatives.

Whether restraint is exercised or not, the volume of labour market information produced and to be processed expeditiously is likely always to show an upward tendency. It is for this reason that the introduction of electronic data processing facilities is likely to receive priority in many developing countries. In most cases, however, cost and skill considerations as well as the availability of sufficient "computerisable" mass, as regards both quantity and quality of data, will counsel a selective and step-by-step installation and use of computer capacity. With the recent advances made in accessibility of micro-computer facilities in terms of cost and skills required, it seems that they provide a suitable means of entry of electronic data processing into labour market information generation and analysis in developing countries. Their primary importance will first of all lie in their potential to speed up data processing and manipulation, now done manually. As a result, manpower projections of the scenario-building type, the construct of manpower accounting models and the timely flow of labour market reporting are likely to be the main beneficiaries. Here again, systematic training of the staff involved is essential.

The improvement of user-producer relations and collaboration, further staff training, particularly at medium technical levels, the fuller exploitation of existing data, a search for operationally more useful manpower and employment information in the informal sector and the gradual introduction of computer facilities into labour market information generation and analysis are likely to form a universally relevant core group of labour market upgrading activities to which priority will be attached in the immediate future, in many developing countries. This core list of desiderata can be clearly deduced from the requests for technical co-operation made by the participants in the regional seminars and in the round-up inter-regional seminar in Copenhagen.

D. The basis of and the priorities for future technical co-operation

Technical co-operation projects in labour market information have been a mixture of activities to reach different sets of objectives, terminating those which had achieved these objectives, applying "more of the same" to those which stubbornly resisted all attempts at improvement and introducing new ones which tried to respond to developments and priorities. It appears useful, therefore, to recall first in a summary fashion what the DANIDA-supported ILO programme to assist developing countries in the upgrading of labour market reporting, of which the five regional seminars and the inter-regional seminar were integral parts, has achieved. During the past ten years of its implementation, there have been clear signs of many-sided progress in labour market information generation in developing countries. However, the rate of progress has often been rather slow and uneven among different components of the programme and among different countries. Moreover, the progress achieved cannot always be directly and fully credited to the programme, in general, and to the regional and inter-regional seminars in particular.

Nevertheless, it can be deduced from many events, facts, statements and indicators that the totality of the diversified efforts undertaken has had visible catalytic effects on progress in labour market information programmes in many developing countries. This was also specifically mentioned by many participants in the seminars. Awareness of the significant role of labour market information as a decision-making instrument, which is useful for many labour market actors, has been well established. So has been the basic knowledge about how to build up comprehensive labour market information programmes, imparted by the exchange of experience at international seminars and through the preparation of guide-lines and manuals by the programme.

In many developing countries the quality of national labour market reporting and of the national state-of-the-art papers prepared for international seminars and workshops on labour market information noticeably increased. Also there was a higher participation rate of higher-level staff with more decision-making responsibilities in national labour market information programmes in subsequent seminars. Apart from a few exceptions, new investments in labour market information upgrading have been modest in scale. However, in some developing countries steps have been taken to make better use of existing resources. Thus, several countries have sought to improve labour market information capacity by a reorientation of staff responsibilities, especially in the employment services. Monographs and papers prepared by the programme have argued for such reorientations and have included manuals setting out guide-lines about how to cope with this task in practice.

Particular efforts were made under the programme to improve the signalling role of labour market information and to extend its role and range to all economic sectors, groups of occupations and regions/areas/localities. Again, a number of manuals and analysis frameworks, as well as numerous articles on labour market signalling, were prepared by the programme to lend support to relevant country attempts.

Technical co-operation activities during the first years of programme implementation were concentrated at the international, regional and subregional levels to ensure the greatest possible impact of the programme. This has led—unintentionally and probably unavoidably—to a certain bias in direction and emphasis of activities in favour of the higher-level echelons of national labour market information personnel. This imbalance is being corrected by the present priority being accorded by the programme to training middle-level technical personnel and staff. Such staff are mainly employed in labour market information activities at subnational, regional and local levels. The recent devolution of planning to these levels, as a result of new policy orientations, has involved greater demands on the planning and operational usefulness of labour market information of regional and local origin. Therefore improvement of skills is of particular importance for this medium-level category of technical staff considering their present inadequate skills, especially for the new tasks expected from them. The programme's response to these newly emerging needs has included the preparation of training guides and manuals, especially for those concerned with the conduct of key informants surveys and subnational manpower analysis.

A considerable number of technical co-operation projects in the fields of manpower planning and labour market information, supported by other resources than those available under the upgrading programme, have been provided with and have made various uses of these technical background documents mentioned above.[9] In return, they have often provided feedback as to their practical use and applicability. This has ensured that programme activities have remained focused on dealing with main issues and problems of labour market information, as experienced by these "field" projects.

Perhaps the most significant, but easily overlooked, achievement of the programme, and notably of the regional seminars, was the fact that the direction and emphasis of the programme was essentially the product of collective thinking of policy-makers, practitioners and, in general, main users of labour market information in developing countries, including the social partners. At the regional seminars, in particular, user needs were clearly articulated in a joint effort—a task which at national levels remains still unresolved in many developing countries.

This rapid assessment should have made it clear that a great deal of groundwork for supporting and underpinning technical co-operation work for upgrading labour market information in developing countries has been completed. The results of this work were made available to many countries to help them put labour market information activities on the road of self-sustaining progress, with and without advice from experts and consultants. Technical co-operation activities of the kind and level pursued under the programme, therefore, do not need continuation *in toto*. However, there remain a number of unresolved and significant key areas where a limited, but strongly focused, ILO programme could provide both effective assistance and catalytic encouragement. These were frequently referred to and emphasised in the discussions of the regional and inter-regional seminars. A broad measure of consensus emerged on the desirability and usefulness of the following types of action.

The first was the continuation of a world-wide ILO effort of studies and research which would concentrate on undertaking conceptual and methodological spadework in labour market information. These activities should seek harmonisation and standardisation of labour market definitions, indicators and data collection, keeping a watch on new labour market information approaches and developments, comparing different country experiences to draw from them relevant lessons and insights and building up a powerhouse of labour market information (data bank) to collect and monitor key labour market indicators world-wide for meeting requests for such information from international and national users.

The second main area of action was the taking of results, lessons and insights gained from the above studies and research to the "field". This would also serve the purpose of instituting a feedback process to ensure relevance and effectiveness of the study and research efforts for technical co-operation. Instead of longer-term resident expertise which formed the backbone of past technical co-operation, this might be more effectively done through the provision of short-term advisory services. These would assist, through repeat missions of short duration, in reviewing and making recommendations, if necessary, for modifications of on-going labour market information programmes or rendering advice on specific aspects or projects of the programme. Such advisory functions, based on essentially short-term expertise which in turn makes it easier to call on high-level consultants, should mainly play a catalytic role. A mandate of this kind should include, as a priority, the fostering of contact and collaboration among main national labour market information users and producers. This should facilitate, through the mechanism of repeat visits, the bringing about of some continuity or even institutional structuring of collaboration, as well as the encouragement of national universities and research institutes to associate themselves with the national labour market information programme.

The third priority area singled out was the support of national training efforts to upgrade the skills of staff and personnel engaged in various positions and with different degrees of responsibility in the broad field of labour market information generation and analysis. It has already been mentioned that stress was to be laid in these efforts on training for medium-level technical personnel. Various conventional training media offered themselves in this respect, including study tours of the workshop type, longer- and shorter-term fellowships, both in developed countries and through technical co-operation between developing countries (TCDC), and participation in special training courses organised by different international or national agencies, institutes or training centres on labour market information or specific aspects of it. One of the priority tasks in this training effort appears to be the training of trainers at the national level to carry the training activities down to the staff categories working at regional and local levels of the labour market information programme. For the training of such trainers detailed courses relevant to particular countries have to be prepared. Available ILO guide-lines and manuals might be used as a starting-point or as a framework for the detailed elaboration of such national programmes. These have to be completed by practical examples of labour market information documentation (studies, reports, surveys, bulletins, etc.) from the country in question to impart knowledge of how labour market information is used to deal with concrete problems. In addition, the translation of ILO guide-lines and manuals in national languages will in many cases be necessary. The development of prototypes of training courses for trainers and their practical application for gaining experience in selected developing countries appears to be the next logical step.

Such a technical co-operation programme to consolidate and continue previous action undertaken to assist developing countries in upgrading their labour market information capacity may give the impression to some that it is not commensurate with the unfinished tasks at hand. Indeed, it is not likely to make dramatic headlines or to stir up much intellectual excitement. In this respect, it shares the fate of other everyday activities which are necessary and even indispensable, but lack lustre and laurels. On the other hand, the programme cannot be considered unrealistic as it is based on the priorities articulated by the "counterparts" of international co-operation and not perceived by the latter. Essentially, it aims at improving their capability of doing labour market research and labour market reporting on their own instead of having this job done by international experts. Last but not least, it does not make extravagant claims on limited—and strained—national and international budgets.

Even on this modest scale, such a technical co-operation programme lends continuity and encouragement to an activity which clearly lies within the ILO's mandate. Therefore, it is bound to render a useful service to all those who need labour market information which is relevant, timely, accurate and of beneficial use for different purposes, at different times, in different forms and in different sequences—this means, practically speaking, to almost everybody. Nevertheless, it is as well to remember that, even bestowed with these qualities, labour market information constitutes merely a basis for informed and rational decision-making in designing and implementing active manpower and employment policies. It is not a substitute for the necessary will and commitment which will finally decide whether the knowledge which good labour market information provides will find translation into such policies.

Notes

[1] Amjad, op. cit., p. 32.

[2] Hollister: *Manpower planning . . .* , op. cit., p. 17.

[3] Dougherty: *Manpower development from three points of view. . .* , op. cit.

[4] An exceptional initial effort of training some 200–300 officials engaged in labour market information activities in French-speaking African countries was undertaken by a series of workshops, especially in Sahelian countries. See J:-B. Célestin. "Manpower planning and labour market information in French-speaking Africa," in *International Labour Review*, July–Aug. 1985.

[5] Chambers, op. cit., p. 99.

[6] C. Salm: *Information and employment policy: General considerations.* IPEA/IPLAN-IBGE-PREALC, Information System for Employment Policy (Brasilia, Sep. 1974), pp. 4–6.

[7] Bienefeld and Godfrey, op. cit., p. 190.

[8] H. Schmitz: *Manufacturing in the backyard* (London, Frances Pinter, 1982).

[9] These guide-lines and manuals include the following main documents: ILO: *Guide-lines for the development of employment and manpower information programmes—A practical manual* (Geneva, 1980); idem: *Employment and manpower information in developing countries—A training guide* (Geneva, 1982); W. Mason and L. Richter: *Reporting by key informants on labour markets* (Geneva, ILO, 1985); and ILO: *Major stages and steps in energy manpower analysis* (Geneva, 1985).

www.ingramcontent.com/pod-product-compliance
Lightning Source LLC
Chambersburg PA
CBHW052106270326
41931CB00012B/2911